eight~wheeled freedom

ALSO BY D. D. MILLER

David Foster Wallace Ruined My Suicide
and Other Stories

eight~wheeled freedom

THE DERBY NERD'S SHORT HISTORY OF FLAT TRACK ROLLER DERBY

dd miller

WOLSAK & WYNN

Cover image: Kevin Konnyu
Cover and interior design: Marijke Friesen
Author photograph: Neil Gunner
Typeset in Miller
Printed by Ball Media, Brantford, Canada

    Canada Council   Conseil des arts
                        for the Arts   du Canada

    ONTARIO ARTS COUNCIL
                        CONSEIL DES ARTS DE L'ONTARIO
                        an Ontario government agency
                        un organisme du gouvernement de l'Ontario

Canadian   Patrimoine
Heritage   canadien

The publisher gratefully acknowledges the support of the Canada Council for the Arts, the Ontario Arts Council and the Canada Book Fund.

Wolsak and Wynn Publishers Ltd.
280 James Street North
Hamilton, ON
Canada L8R 2L3

Library and Archives Canada Cataloguing in Publication

Miller, D. D., 1976-, author
     Eight-wheeled freedom : the derby nerd's short history of flat track roller derby / D.D. Miller.

ISBN 978-1-928088-13-4 (paperback)

1. Roller derby—History. 2. Women roller skaters—History.
3. Feminism and sports. I. Title.

GV859.6.M54 2016   796.21082   C2016-900682-4

This one's for Dawson.

"The history of women in sport is a history of cultural resistance."
– M. Ann Hall, *The Girl and the Game*

TABLE OF CONTENTS

prologue

My relationship with the game of flat track roller derby changed forever on November 5, 2010, in Chicago, Illinois.

Up until that time, my understanding of the modern version of the sport had been limited to community-level, DIY, local derby. This was a sport played in rec centres and iceless neighbourhood hockey arenas in the spring and summer months by brave, interesting (and not always athletic) women. Women who, for the most part, defied a single demographic placement, although on the surface there were a lot of tattoos, a lot of dyed hair and a clear queer-positive aesthetic.

By the end of 2010, I'd been swept up in the flat track revolution for a few years and I had watched many games in those iceless arenas in Montreal, Hamilton, Kitchener, London, Ottawa and Toronto. I'd had to set aside a new space in my closet just for roller derby T-shirts and my partner had become a skater on the Death Track Dolls, a house league team in Toronto. I'd begun to write fairly regularly about the sport, took road trips just to see games, had done some online colour commentary and play-by-play in Montreal, and was lined up to announce Toronto's locally televised house league championship game. I even had a derby name. Basically, I was as big a Canadian fan of roller derby as you could find. But even in the comparative isolation of the Canadian roller derby scene, I could tell something was changing that fall.

When Drew Barrymore's roller derby revival film, *Whip It*, had premiered at the Toronto International Film Festival (TIFF) a year before, I'd seen thousands of people cram Yonge-Dundas Square in downtown Toronto to rub shoulders with the film's stars and watch an exhibition roller derby game. Although the film dealt with a small, independent, banked track league in Austin, Texas, after the film's release, North American women of all ages were Googling *roller derby*, finding their nearest flat track league and buying fresh meat gear packages from the handful of derby retailers selling them at the time.

The larger community that supported the game was just beginning to open up to Canadians. Within the past year, both Montreal and Hamilton had become the first non-US-based members of the Women's Flat Track Derby Association (WFTDA). Though still in its infancy, the WFTDA ran the closest thing the sport had to a professional league, annually organizing its members into four ten-team regional playoff tournaments, where teams vied for an opportunity to play in what had until then been called the National Championship Tournament.

Montreal, and its cheekily named travel team – The New Skids on the Block – turned heads in its first year playing within the association by qualifying for the Eastern Region playoffs. It was an appearance that had forced the WFTDA to rethink its marketing and its terminology as the game had clearly burst forth from the US border. *Nationals*, for example, became *Championships*, although in 2010 most people called them *Championals*.

With the rise of sites like The Derby News Network (DNN), Derby Tron and Flat Track Stats, I could now follow along with the growing rivalries of the sport's top teams, and I was getting to know the key skaters and the slowly expanding star system that resides at the heart of any sport. Glued to my computer screen and the Derby News Network's expanding broadcast of the regional playoffs (*boutcast* in derby lingo), my understanding of the game and the breadth of its growth was expanding rapidly. I'd become a big enough fan of the game that when I heard that Champs were going to be held in Chicago that year, I jumped at the opportunity to see the sport played at its highest level and by its best practitioners.

So on November 5, 2010, I walked into the UIC Pavilion in Chicago for day one of the 2010 WFTDA Championship (nicknamed Uproar on the Lakeshore). Although it was early on in the tournament, there were thousands of fans crammed into the lower bowl of the Pavilion. Vendors were hawking their wares on the concourse, and beer and popcorn sellers were squeezing their way through the face-painted, sign-sporting fans in the seats. It was like walking into any North American sporting event, only in the centre of it all was a blue sport-court flat track, and skating around it were two roller derby teams. The B.ay A.rea D.erby Girls (from San Francisco and the Bay Area) and Austin's already legendary Texecutioners, the founders of the modern revival, were well into the first game of the tournament. In the end, Texas took a low-scoring victory in what was an incredibly tough defensive game, but I barely noticed. I spent most of that first day staring in amazement, my neck swivelling in wide circles, attempting to take it all in. To figure out what it all meant.

This was big-arena roller derby, being played in a venue and for a crowd that was unprecedented in the seven years since the revival of the sport. The beer was overpriced and the concessions were awful. Some of the fans were obnoxious, belligerent, even had their bodies painted. There were mascots and loud music and half-time shows and vendor stations and everything else that you would expect to find at a North American sporting event.

I was not alone in making my pilgrimage-style march from north of the border to the 2010 WFTDA Championship, and I was not alone in having a life-changing moment at the event either, although it probably didn't coalesce as nicely as I like to remember it. But I came to some realizations that weekend. Thoughts that I'd been having about the sport – the state of the game, its role in my life and the world and the future of it; thoughts that every roller derby skater and superfan have probably had – were finally forming into something coherent. I was seeing the early stages of the twenty-first century (at least from a Western perspective) playing out in women's flat track roller derby. It was a fully wired, Internet-driven, grassroots (yet increasingly global), non-partisan, anti-judgmental women's revolution. I don't want to sound too hyperbolic, but in the simplest way I realized that modern flat track roller derby had grown so beyond its roots that it was here to stay.

This was something that had never been taken for granted before. Everyone – even my grandmother – was aware of roller derby's semi-dubious history, its ebbs and flows and shifts and alterations. Its languishing in the dregs of sports entertainment. No matter what the incarnation, roller derby had never lasted, always vanishing when the novelty of that latest spectacle waned. But buoyed by social media and the rise of web streaming, from 2003 to 2010 the flat track version of the sport had grown by nearly 1500 per cent. It had gone from a kitschy, loosely organized, punk rock–inspired third-wave feminist movement to a global competitive sporting phenomenon played in nearly twenty countries and counting.

And in Chicago that weekend, beginning when I first walked into the Pavilion and ending when Denver's Rocky Mountain Rollergirls were in the midst of a last-moment comeback that would see them defeat the defending champion, Oly Rollers, it became clear to me that roller derby had grown well beyond Austin's Texas Rollergirls. It had grown beyond all of the skaters in Chicago that weekend, the thousands of fans in the building, the many more tuning in to DNN for live coverage. It also became clear to me that when we were all gone, the sport would not be. Flat track roller derby would be played by someone else and watched by countless others – changed, tinkered with, made better – but whatever was going to happen and whatever the future held, for the first time in its somewhat troubled history, I knew without a doubt that this time roller derby was not going to fade away.

a wholly unique music

THE CALL OF THE FLAT TRACK

May 31, 2008. Montreal, QC

The streets were so empty we could hear the sounds of our shoes scuffing the sidewalk, kicking up dust created by the remarkably dry, warm spring air. We were rushing down St-Dominique Street in Montreal's Mile End neighbourhood, late, and up ahead we could see our destination. Arena Saint-Louis was nondescript, a squat-looking brick arena that wouldn't look out of place in any city, town or village in Canada, and it seemed silent from a distance, empty perhaps. I was starting to wonder if we'd even come to the right place. But once we stood at the foot of the steps leading up to the main entrance we could hear it: a faint din leaking out through the glass doors at the top of the stairs; the muffled moans of a crowd; the sharp voice of an announcer cutting through a blanket of sound. We hurried up the steps, our hands slipping from each other's grasp.

Entering the door we gave our tickets to a young woman with a thick nose ring. Tattoos of paws scampered up her left forearm, her hair was an asymmetrical, spiky blue, but she had a sweet smile and welcomed us in slightly accented English. She ushered us through the inner doors and we found ourselves on a concourse overlooking a bowled arena with a wall of seats immediately beneath us.

It was packed, as packed as this small Canadian arena could be, and loud: the acoustics of the building allowing the sound to rebound, echo and erupt as they would for any sporting event. Only the crowd was unlike any I'd ever seen downtown at the Bell Centre watching the Habs. It was mostly women, for one, and predominantly lesbian, I assumed: heavily tattooed, pierced and as equally decked out in armless, punk rock–certified fraying jean jackets as they were in hipster-chic skinny jeans and retro plaid. It was a glorious sea of riled up, belligerent fans, screaming at the action below with their hands thrust skyward, clutching half-drunk cans of Pabst Blue Ribbon (PBR). I followed those cries down onto the arena floor – iceless now – to an oval in the centre of the polished concrete, marked out by pink duct tape over a rope and ringed by a circle of fans three-rows deep, who either sat directly on the floor or stood, leaning over those sitting, straining to have their voices heard on the track where two groups of women roller skated.

The action on the track that they were all so focused on was a blur to me, a swirl of purples and greens and blacks, hair whipping out from under helmets, arms flailing, bodies tumbling, a cacophony of seemingly uncontrolled chaos. Over it all, I could hear a single voice cutting through the noise with a crisp timbre that focused my attention. Standing in the centre of the oval, seemingly flitting above the mess of bodies that surrounded or scrambled upon the track, was a stunning human. A topless feminine figure, confidently decked out in very little: high-heeled black leather boots that stretched up to the knee and gave way to smooth, toned thighs, black booty shorts and a matte-black corset that thrust and presented the figure's masculine, muscular chest upward toward a perfectly contoured face. The face – sharp, deep-cheeked, with smoky charcoal around the eyes giving them an enigmatic, yet still penetrating look – was framed by a shiny platinum bob that cut a line of straight bangs above the brow. The announcer strutted about the action, drifting effortlessly between English and French, sometimes interacting directly with the crowd and seemed to be describing the sight in some carnivalized version of a traditional sports play-by-play. As I listened I began to see – ever so crudely – the links between the action and the words. The chaos on the track seemed to slow somewhat, at least to the point where I could distinguish one team from another and the skaters from each other. I began to see the slight consistency in the uniforms, but mostly I was taken by the personalized variations: the heavily stickered helmets, multicoloured knee and elbow pads, the fishnets or booty shorts. I may not have understood the game, but at least I recognized the sport of roller derby.

I wish I could remember what my expectations were for that night, but whatever they may have been, I know they were wrong. It's probably more accurate to say my expectations were shapeless and weighed down by murky memories of a dead sport. I would quickly learn that the state of the game was in a similar spot, that the muddle I was seeing and feeling was actually the murkiness of a game trying to figure itself out.

My partner, Jan Dawson, and I were nearing the end of our time in Montreal. We'd been in the city for two years while she completed her graduate degree in Library and Information Studies at McGill University. We had been tipped off about Montreal's roller derby league from two of her classmates who were budding fans. We were supposed to meet them that night, but our late arrival made finding them difficult. So instead, we grabbed a couple cans of PBR (two for five dollars) and headed to where a few seats remained in the southern edge of the stands. As the first game neared its end, Montreal's defending house league champions, Les Filles du Roi, were on the wrong side of the score against a team from Boston called the B Party. In the buildup to the evening, I had naively thought that flat track roller derby was exclusively a Montreal thing, so I watched enthralled as these women who had travelled all the way from Boston rocked the Montreal skaters. As the night wore on and the pyramids of empty PBR cans began to rise along the side of the track (they were called *beeramids* I would later learn, built in the hopes of being knocked down by a skater hit out of bounds), the crowd became increasingly belligerent toward the opposition, and downright rude and obnoxious toward the referees.

For someone like me – a slightly nerdy, but passionate sports fan, who'd played a few sports, but would never have been considered a jock at any point in his life – being in that arena that night felt like being in a kind of paradise. Here was a sport that had many of the trappings of the traditional sports spectacle but managed to feel completely different. From its competitors – women who ranged widely in size, shape, sexuality and style – to its announcer to its fans, nothing seemed recognizable to me, a lifetime consumer of the Big Four North American sports and the bloated amateurism of the Olympics. One thing that remained the same was that core of sports empathy that is nearly inde-scribable and that people seem to crave once they get a taste for it: the joining together with a group of others and rallying behind a team. I could feel it there that night immediately, even if whatever was happening on the floor in front of me was unlike any sport I had ever seen and the audience surrounding me was unlike any I'd ever been in.

Walking into Montreal's Arena Saint-Louis is for fans of Canadian roller derby what walking into the old Montreal Forum would have been for fans of hockey. After the closing of Edmonton's Grindhouse (a.k.a. the Metro Sportsplex) in the summer of 2014, Arena Saint-Louis became the single oldest continuously used arena for roller derby in Canada, and some of the defining moments for the sport in this country have happened there. In May 2008, Montreal Roller Derby was in the early stages of its second competitive season. I was surprised to discover that the league consisted of about sixty women, separated onto three home (or house league) teams: Les Contrabanditas, La Racaille and Les Filles du Roi. The top sixteen or so skaters had also recently formed the all-star team, The New Skids on the Block.

Jan and I saw every game that season, never leaving our spots at turn 1 of the trackside suicide seats. We saw the regular season and the playoffs. On July 12, we watched our first Canadian inter-league game between Montreal's New Skids and Hamilton's Hammer City Eh! Team, where I realized, for the first time, that this sport was being played elsewhere in Canada. All of this was to come, but on that initial night in May, I remember Jan and I glancing at each other in silent wonderment. Once we'd gained some confidence, we began to ask the fans around us about certain aspects of the game, but we quickly discovered that not many in the audience really knew what was going on. Many had seen the sport only once or twice before, or, more often than not, not at all. The best we got was that there were three positions: the blockers, the pivot (who was a blocker that wore a stripe on her helmet, the reasoning for it beyond my understanding at the time) and the jammer, the skater who could score points and who had a star on her helmet.

By the second game of that first evening's doubleheader, I was starting to figure things out, at least on a large scale. The sprawling mass of what seemed to be pure confusion began to take on shape, and I could see a little order to the commotion. And, like most of the people who have leapt into twenty-first century roller derby, particularly in those first years when it was still essentially unknown and you could stumble unaware into an unassuming neighbourhood arena and discover this thriving, raucous subculture, I had what some skaters refer to as "the calling." Most skaters, announcers and officials are able to boil their callings down to a specific moment. A moment when the sounds and sensations create an almost out-of-body experience that allows something small and specific to suddenly open up to expose an all-encompassing bigger picture.

This calling doesn't happen as much anymore because that element of being caught off guard has been lost. Even if people don't quite know exactly what it is, everyone seems to know that there is a roller derby revival going on, so the sport surprises people less and less. But when it was still a derby little secret hidden away in rinks and gyms in a few places across North America, the discovery was often a shocking revelation. The first few waves of the growth of the sport consisted of women having this calling and following it to extremes. In Canada in 2007 and early 2008, there were only a few cities where derby was played – Montreal, Toronto, Hamilton, Edmonton and Vancouver – so at this stage the future roller girls who would soon take up the game in London, Ottawa, Kitchener-Waterloo, Red Deer and Victoria relied on the existence of those initial leagues to discover the sport.

The moment of my calling came late on that first night in Arena Saint-Louis. Fuelled by equal parts wonder, adrenaline and beer, it was life altering.

It turned out that both Montreal teams were quite over-matched (I would learn later that the US teams were significantly more experienced), but in the second game, featuring La Racaille taking on Female Trouble, a team from Baltimore, I finally began to notice that whenever one particular skater took to the track wearing a helmet cover with a star on it, La Racaille's score rose. She was easy to pick out as she skated with an awkward, hunched-over stride that brought her so low around the turns she could slap the floor if she wanted. She gave me something to latch on to and gaining a centre point allowed me to see that there was an order to things. There were strategies and counter-strategies. I could match the cheers in the crowd with this skater's ability to get through the pack, weave her way through the opposing blockers and take assists from her own.

The skater's name, I learned quickly, was the Iron Wench.

As Iron Wench approached the track and one of her teammates knocked an opposition blocker out of the way so she could get past, the sport began to unfold for me. It was a raw understanding, though the sport at the time was still in a fairly raw state, but when that fundamental understanding of the game coupled with the energy in the arena that night, I knew I was falling in love with the game. Luckily, when I looked over at Jan, I saw that something had changed in her as well. She was the one who would first describe to me the moment of her own calling. Later she told me that as soon as she walked into the arena, she felt as if she were surrounded by her "people," though she couldn't explain with any more precision who those people were.

As La Racaille's loss at the hands of Baltimore was winding down, we began to anticipate when Iron Wench would come back on the track. We could easily recognize her loose gait, the rounded back and the jutting elbows. Eventually I began to look beyond her stance and down at her feet. When I'd first walked in, the tangle of legs and knee pads had been a blur, but late in the second game, I could begin to make out the skates – all quad roller skates, of course – cutting through the air. They almost seemed to be floating above the concrete. Then I finally heard the sound, the muffled screech of wheel edges connecting, digging into the concrete underneath. It was unlike anything I'd heard before, maybe similar to an ice skate stopping sharply, digging into ice and kicking up a spray of snow and ice bits, but it was deeper, heavier. It was as if the hard plastic wheels were sanding down the concrete, grinding it away to nothing; and the more the skaters moved their feet – stopped, started, leapt, turned – the more the wheels would screech. It was unnerving. It was mesmerizing. It was a wholly unique music, and I was hooked.

by the skater, for the skater

THE DO-IT-YOURSELF DRIVE BEHIND THE CANADIAN ROLLER DERBY REVIVAL

It's game day at the Bunker, the home of Toronto Roller Derby (ToRD) since fall 2011, an old military supply depot in Downsview Park just north of downtown Toronto. The Bunker is swarming with activity, with dozens of volunteers at work, virtually all of them players whose teams are not scheduled to play tonight, but also spouses (who are often labelled derby widows if they don't get involved) and other family members. Some of these volunteers set up temporary changing rooms in one end of the building over what is known as track 2; other skaters work to shore up the thin roped track outline around track 1 as volunteers use large brooms to sweep around them, removing any fine debris from the track. Still more are lining the track with movable steel bleachers, rolling them into place on their stiff, tired wheels, while a few others set up the bar. Roller skating and derby-specific vendors are putting up temporary shops in vendor alley; the ToRD.TV crew is taping down cables from the cameras lining the track and preparing for the evening's live web-streamed broadcast; and, of course, somewhere in amongst all this, there are skaters warming up for their game.

The Bunker is a massive space, lined throughout with thick concrete columns that guide you through the dusty room. It is windowless; the only natural light that makes its way into the building is through a garage door at the far end, near where the members of ToRD were able to craftily set up one of the two flat track roller derby tracks in the space. Although it doesn't have the sort of seminal history that Edmonton's Grindhouse or Montreal's Arena Saint-Louis have, during its time as ToRD's home, the Bunker has been the busiest roller derby space in Canada, and one of the busiest in the world. Nine or ten teams spread over three leagues use the space, with all seven of ToRD's teams practicing on weeknights (the multiple tracks allow two teams a night to practice). On Saturday afternoons when there aren't any games to set up for, full league practice is held. On Sundays, the busiest day of the week, Toronto Junior Roller Derby and Toronto Men's Roller Derby share the space with the skaters of ToRD's Fresh Meat Training Program.

It is as far from a traditional sports venue as you will find; a repurposed, inadequate space (setting up a round track surrounding huge pillars *should* be impossible) made to not only work, but to thrive. Skating in the Bunker is the personification of the Women's Flat Track Derby Association's "by the skater, for the skater" mantra, a perfect illustration of the do-it-yourself approach that has driven the flat track revival of roller derby.

In her expansive and inclusive 2005 book *DIY: The Rise of Lo-Fi Culture*, Amy Spencer charts the history of the DIY ethos, as she calls it, from its roots in sci-fi fanzines in the 1930s and the beat generation's self-publishing of the '50s to its defining moments with the '70s punk and the '90s riot grrrl movements.

In the introduction, Spencer points out that across DIY subcultures "the primary aim is to build unique idealized networks in which anyone can participate" (11) and that participants in DIY culture are driven by "the urge to create a new cultural form and transmit it to others on [their] own terms" (12). When discussing the riot grrrl movement, which derby rose from, Spencer notes that the movement sprouted in the early '90s from women's dissatisfaction with the dominant indie culture of the time: "Many young women did not see themselves represented in either the mainstream music or the underground [i.e., grunge] in the early '90s" (292), and because of this, "they wanted to break away from the preconceived stereotypes of female sexuality in rock music" (293). Although Spencer's study was published in 2005 during the earliest days of the development of the roller derby revival – 2005 was the year that the WFTDA formed – the sport could have slipped easily into her book.

Just as the early riot grrrls in the '90s saw no place for themselves in the dominant music scene, a large swath of women saw no place for themselves in mainstream sports, despite seeming advancement in women's athletics. Whether it was the playing of a feminized version of a "man's" game or the perpetuation of stereotypical notions of female beauty advanced by mainstream sports, many women did not see a place for themselves within the culture. Travis Beaver, a University of Texas at Austin researcher who has studied roller derby's DIY ethos, concludes that the roller derby revival's do-it-yourself approach was born not only out of necessity, but that it was also a value ingrained in the very philosophical underpinnings of the sport (36) and continues to be a guiding principle. The WFTDA, while putting strict regulations around gameplay, has no rules in terms of organization, save one: it requires member leagues to be owned and operated by the skaters. How the league is organized (the number of teams, as a business or non-profit, for example) is strictly up to the league itself. So in many ways "DIY derby" has become institutionalized and this organizational freedom is seen as a way of maintaining controlling interest of the sport. It also inspires a level of investment in the game that extends well beyond the action on the track.

At the time of the sport's birth in Canada, and the rest of the world outside the US as well, the participants were in it as much for the cultural and social aspects as they were for the sport. The equal footing of the culture around the game and the game itself was also a big part of the riot grrrl movement and the do-it-yourself ethos as a whole. Amy Spencer notes that riot grrrl wasn't only about music and argues that "it asserted itself as both a social and cultural movement. Adapting theories of third wave feminism into everyday life" (294). The early twenty-first century roller girls are an embodiment of this notion.

As women swarmed to flat track roller derby, it was for much more than the sport. It was for the freedom that the cultural space surrounding it promised, it was for the knowledge that whatever kind of woman you were – you could be a homemaker, you could be a punk rock shit disturber – in a roller derby space you would not only be welcomed, but you would be celebrated. It was this sense of ownership and empowerment that directly spurred the growth of the game. For the same reasons that women flocked to read Kathleen Hanna's *Riot Grrrl Manifesto* in the early '90s (initially released in her self-published zine), they flocked to read the WFTDA rule set in the early to mid 2000s. In roller derby, as in riot grrrl, the participants saw themselves as "manufacturers of culture" and not "participants in a culture that they were forced to accept" (Spencer, 49). Travis Beaver describes this desire for control as a way of avoiding the kind of "alienation that occurs when the means of production are privately owned and controlled" (38). The roller derby revival is unique in the world of sport where some variation of the hierarchical owner-manager-coach-player stratification is the standard operating model.

While the sport would find a foothold in England, Germany, Australia and New Zealand that year as well, beginning in 2006, Canada became roller derby's "second country." In only a few years' time the nation exploded with the sport, nurturing leagues all across the country, in its biggest cities and smallest towns. In 2006 that DIY ethos at the heart of derby gripped women in five cities, the all important "first five" of Canadian Roller Derby: Montreal, Toronto, Hamilton, Edmonton and Vancouver.

1. Southern Ontario (Hamilton and Toronto)

Hamilton, Ontario, a rugged steel town with deep working-class roots, is a city on the cusp of change. Traditionally, it has been a football town, sporting one of the Canadian Football League's most beloved organizations: the Tiger Cats. The Ticats, being the only pro game in the city – or anywhere in the region outside of Toronto for that matter – is a team loved with a fervour that is common to small cities with big teams. Think Green Bay, Wisconsin (the NFL's Packers); Regina, Saskatchewan (CFL's Roughriders); San Antonio, Texas (NBA's Spurs); Winnipeg, Manitoba (NHL's Jets); or any small American college town with a National Collegiate Athletic Association (NCAA) basketball or football team.

Hamilton, perhaps given its proximity to the increasingly expensive metropolis of Toronto, has seen a boom in the second decade of the twenty-first century. With the steel and other industries that once sustained it slipping into decline, there has been a recent movement of artists and writers heading there for the cheap rent and the community-like feel of a city that still has all of the comforts that one could want. In late winter 2006, Hamilton's Corktown Pub was also the scene of one of the first meetings of women ready to play flat track roller derby in Canada.

Not that the sport had never been played on Canadian soil: it had. And not that Canadian women had never had an impact on the game either: they had.

From about 1935 to 1972, the game of roller derby was a banked track sport run exclusively by the Seltzer family. Starting with father Leo, son Jerry would eventually take over the running and development of the game in 1959. Jerry says that his father always thought that with our speed-skating culture, Canada could and should be a prime breeding ground for future skaters. Leo had seen that potential first hand. During its initial rise as an endurance sport, one of the first stars of what was then called Transcontinental Roller Derby (and still a racing-based sport) was a Canadian speed skater named Ivy King, who at one point held records in multiple distances (Storms, 75). Later, in the late '60s, another Canadian star became central to the sport: Quebec's Francine Cochu won rookie of the year in 1967 and was a key skater in Seltzer derby through to its end (Coppage, 46). However, the sport first made its way to Canada before Cochu's time (and after King's). It did so shortly after Jerry took over the running of the league from his father.

The first game of roller derby in Canada was played in Sudbury, Ontario, as part of a short tour of Seltzer's derby in 1961. The tour was to go from Sudbury to Ottawa, down to Toronto and then across to Montreal. It was a forgettable tour save for one interesting bit of history that only in retrospect seems significant:

It was during this tour that *flat* track roller derby made its debut in Canada.

At the time, the teams travelled separately from the massive banked track that had to be lugged around on the tours. The morning after the game in Sudbury, the truck carrying the track froze, delaying it significantly. The players, who'd forged ahead and were waiting in Ottawa for their playing surface to arrive, eventually realized that the track was not going to show up in time. They decided to play anyway. However, after awkwardly skating around the flat surface for a while, Jerry says, they eventually cancelled the game and the event in Ottawa. "We all agreed," he reminisced during a 2010 interview, "you couldn't skate roller derby on a flat surface" ("Jerry Seltzer 2010 WFTDA Champs").

But by 2006, as roller derby was about to spread across the country of Canada, the game was virtually played only on a flat surface.

There was a mixed allure to the game in 2006, without much focus on strategy in the sport. Basically, skaters were taught to skate fast and turn left. A lot of the training in those early days of the game was focused on skating nearly exclusively: how to use the multiple edges that the four-wheeled quads have, how to stop and how to fall properly after taking a hit. The sport, at the time, lacked strategic sophistication, so the spectators – and a lot of time even the skaters – had little clue as to what was going on. The game was, and still remains, simple enough at its core. One of the team's designated skaters – the jammer – is supposed to lap opponents for points. Early on in the flat track game, there was essentially no strategy beyond hitting hard, staying upright and keeping your jammer in front of the opposing jammer long enough for your jammer to get points. It was a straightforward, at times brutal, game. And when a certain type of woman found it, it was entrancing.

For many women in these early days of Canadian roller derby who lacked a flesh and blood precedent, the call to the flat track came after tuning in to A&E's short-lived winter 2006 TV show about the roller derby revival called *Rollergirls*, which is exactly what inspired Whiplasha (a.k.a. Lasha Laskowsky-Reed), a Mc-Master University student and punk band singer, to write an email to a handful of her friends about the possibility of forming a league in Hamilton. At the inaugural meeting at the Cork-town, sixteen women showed up, immediately agreeing to found a league starting with one of our country's now most venerable roller derby teams: the Hamilton Harlots.

The name embodies much of that early spirit of roller derby: the punk rock, ironic irreverence that was at its core. But in an interview with the *Hamilton Spectator* Lasha explained that the somewhat controversial name, while it was supposed to be "edgy and sexy," was not demeaning. She strained to make it clear that "we're not the Harlots, the whores. We're the Harlots, the troublemakers" (quoted in Borcea).

But it did ride that fine line that this first wave of Canadian roller derby grappled with. While the depth and persistence of the revival finally has people altering their attitudes about what roller derby is, in 2006 the new players were dealing with both a decades-old stigma and a perception that the new game was little more than a titillating, sexy throwback to an old form of sports entertainment. But by the time the revival had made its way to Canada, through the formation of the WFTDA, flat track roller derby had already established itself as a legitimate, competitive sport and was on the cusp of hosting its first national championship. So while the women getting involved in that first wave certainly didn't fear playing up the sexier aspects of a sport that could be described as chicks on roller skates bodychecking each other (evidenced by the amount of fishnet stockings that remained in the Canadian game through to 2009/2010), right from the start there was a sense that this was going to be a sport, not a spectacle.

If the name of Hamilton's first team spoke to one side of the roller derby coin, the name of the second spoke to the other.

As more and more women began to show an interest in the city's new game, the skaters formed a second team, and it was named the Steel Town Tank Girls, a nod to both the steel-based working-class roots of the city, as well as the third-wave feminist undercurrent that carried much of the first generation of skaters in the twenty-first century roller derby revival. *Tank Girl* was a counterculture, punk-feminist '80s comic that became an image of a certain type of rebellion in the '90s. The character herself was an unapologetic over-sexual, hyper-violent woman immortalized by Lori Petty in the 1995 film adaptation. Tank Girl became a symbol of the general counterculture movement in the '90s, but especially of the riot grrrl movement, and was wrapped up as well in the queer movements of the time. Steel Town Tank Girls may have been the perfect name for a roller derby team from Hamilton.

Meanwhile, not far east up Highway 403, the city of Toronto was already home to one online roller skate retailer: RollerBug Skate Co.

Alyson McMullen started RollerBug in 2005 after a fruitless search for roller skates in Toronto. Interested in roller skating and not aware of roller derby, Alyson started working with Dominion Skate Company to make a more modern skate and developed a quad that was a little shorter than traditional artistic skates and featured open-toed boots. Unknowingly, her design was very similar to the skates being worn by derby skaters south of the border. Things started slowly for the company, but the number of orders that came in from women in the US quickly surprised Alyson. She would eventually figure out that they were playing roller derby.

Her first online search for women's roller derby took her to the website of Seattle's Rat City Rollergirls, one of the first flat track leagues in the world. To this day Alyson remembers the first time she saw their logo: it's a saucy, cartoony girl; the view is side-on but just the upper body, and her head is turned outward, arched downward just slightly. She's got shoulder-length, black, pin-up-style hair and is sporting a massive black eye.

"I remember seeing the logo with the black eye and thinking 'What is this?' Their aesthetic was very riot grrrly, which was amazing to me," she says. "I don't know if I thought too far into it at the time, but that aesthetic was what initially sparked my interest." Alyson put up a notice on the RollerBug website asking any Toronto-based women if they were interested in starting a roller derby team. Responses were slow to trickle in. Eventually, Alyson reached out to another Canadian retailer of roller skates, Vancouver's Lisa Suggitt, who ran Rollergirl.ca, to inquire about roller derby, but although Suggitt was also selling skates and equipment to derby skaters from the American west coast, there'd yet to be any movement on starting a team in Vancouver.

It took six months for RollerBug to receive ten messages about roller derby from women in Toronto, but that was enough for Alyson. In the winter of 2006, with posters for A&E's *Rollergirls* lining bus shelters and splattered on billboards, a dozen interested women met at the Armadillo Texas Grill in downtown Toronto to discuss the possibility of starting a team. Although it would take a few more months to organize their first practice in spring 2006 at the neglected Coachlite Roller Rink in Oshawa in the far eastern reaches of the Greater Toronto Area, the young team quickly agreed on a name: the Smoke City Betties.

Interestingly enough, across the city, there was another team brewing independently from the Betties, the Toronto Terrors. Like Whiplasha in Hamilton, one of the Terrors co-founders, Monica Mitchell (a.k.a. Monichrome), was also inspired by *Rollergirls* to form not only a team but a whole league. There were five key figures in the first meeting and within months, the core organizers had developed a league model (with the idea of having four distinct teams) and had designated captains and an unelected executive to lead the way. The executive featured two men: Scooter, the primary force behind the Terrors, and Trevor Welsch, Monichrome's partner at the time. But it would also feature a skater president (Sanderella), Monichrome as secretary/treasurer and another skater, Mia Culprit, who was in charge of media, and who, interestingly enough, would many years later, in 2015, be hired in a marketing role as one of the few WFTDA full-time staff members.

While the Smoke City Betties headed to Coachlite for their first practices, the Terrors went west to suburban Mississauga's Scooter's Roller Palace, which brought roller derby to both of the GTA's remaining roller rinks. The first tryouts for the Terrors happened on a Sunday in April and featured sixty potential skaters, nearly all of whom were selected to one of the four teams, then named the Death Track Dolls, Chicks Ahoy!, D-VAS (Deadly Viper Assassination Squad) and the Bay Street Bruisers.

Back in Hamilton, the Tank Girls and the Harlots were now under the umbrella of a league they called the Hammer City Roller Girls. Hammer is a common nickname of the city, but the name was also inspired by members of the Hamilton music scene – so vital to the initial growth of the derby scene – who were often called Hammer Rockers. The stage was set for the first official flat track roller game to be played in the country. On Saturday, July 22, 2006, at a sold out Burlington arena, the Hamilton Harlots and the Steel Town Tank Girls welcomed the sport of roller derby back to Canada. It would be the only public house league game played in the country that year, although there'd be a ground breaking international showdown out west later, and it was a resounding success. Over one thousand fans crammed the arena that night, a crowd that included many members of the Terrors and the Betties. There were rock bands, a local beer sponsor and cheerleaders. For the record, the final score of that game was the Tank Girls, 83, and the Harlots, 68, but most importantly, roller derby was reborn and modern flat track roller derby was officially in Canada.

Given the success of Hammer City's opening game, which many aspiring Toronto players had gone to see, a debate began among the Betties about also playing in public, with half wanting to and the other half concerned that they weren't ready. As a compromise, it was decided that they would host a semi-closed tournament, or a day of derby, featuring a series of mini-games with the winner crowned Derby Queens of the Pre-Season. These Derby Queens would then take on the host Betties in a full-length regulation contest; most importantly, an after-party was scheduled for Toronto's Bovine Sex Club with bands and door prizes. Interestingly, while the Betties would not charge to go to the arena to watch the game, tickets were sold for the after-party, which had a post-riot-grrrl feel featuring bands like Cougar Party (billed on the poster as "all-girl DIY fiery PUNK"), the Carbonas and the Punching Nuns.

Seen as much as a learning and sharing experience as a competitive endeavour, the Betties took the opportunity to invite the Terrors, who had already divided and developed the structure of Toronto Roller Derby by then. Using connections made at Scooter's Roller Palace, where Hamilton players often skated, they also invited along the Hammer City Roller Girls. Through early message boards, the Toronto skaters also became aware of groups of women organizing in Montreal, Edmonton and Vancouver, and passed on invitations to them. For cost and organizational reasons, the western skaters declined the invite, but although they had yet to name their league or teams, Montreal signed up. For the skaters of Toronto and Montreal, the one-day tournament was about developing strategies and skills, and playing in a bouting or game situation for the first time. It was presented as such, marketed directly to the women as an opportunity "to meet fellow derby sisters, learn and share drills, and exchange skating tips."

On August 19, 2006, the Smoke City Betties hosted D-Day at George Bell Arena in downtown Toronto's west end, and the formation of the Canadian roller derby community began.

"I don't remember much about it," admits Alyson, then known as Kandy Barr. "I remember it being a blur mostly, and I remember Hamilton being really good."

The importance of this tournament in terms of the development of roller derby in Eastern Canada cannot be overstated. D-Day was essential in spreading the sport, giving skaters a chance to learn everything from the organizational know-how needed to run a game right down to the skills and footwork necessary to employ the early basic strategies of the sport. For many of the skaters there, despite having skated for months, it would be the first time they had ever seen a flat track roller derby game played.

On the track, Hammer City, not surprisingly, dominated, eventually defeating one of the Montreal teams in the final of the tournament (43–10 in the mini-game) and then the Betties in the full-length main event (79–57).

This was also an important event off the track, as it sparked the inspiration for a merger between the Betties (who also birthed a second team, the Gore-Gore Rollergirls, shortly after D-Day) and the new Toronto league, briefly making ToRD the largest roller derby league in North America. On the track, Hammer City made it clear that they were going to be the early competitive leaders in this part of the country, but Montreal – nameless still – also surprised with their ability, which provided a certain kind of foreshadowing for the dominant league they would quickly create.

2. Montreal

On Friday, March 3, 2006, six months before the Betties' D-Day, somebody going by the handle MissTheMeaner posted a message in Rollergirl.ca's online roller skating forum with the subject line "Rollerderby in Montreal." She asked, simply, if anyone was interested in becoming part of a roller derby team in the city. The post got exactly one response, seventeen days later, from someone posting as Georgia W. Tush: "i am! i am!! so bad it hurts."

In 2006, Georgia W. Tush (a.k.a. Alyssa Kwasny) had just moved to the big city of Montreal from Thunder Bay in rural northern Ontario to study at Concordia University. An organizer in Thunder Bay's music scene, she found herself running in the same circles in Montreal. As she says, she "was broke, went to shows and partied. I felt a bit lost."

Alyssa hadn't seen the TV show *Rollergirls* at the time, but, early in 2006, a friend of her husband's who lived in Chicago joined one of that city's roller derby leagues. The notion intrigued her, although she admits that she initially thought it would just be an opportunity to get more involved in the rockabilly scene, but Kwasny quickly discovered that there was no roller derby league in Montreal. Indeed, her early Internet snooping led her to the realization that there were no roller derby leagues in Canada. She did find MySpace pages and websites for leagues south of the border and, like Alyson McMullen in Toronto, was immediately taken in by the imagery. On MySpace, "it was mostly photos of girls partying and holding up roller skates! Perfect!" she remembers thinking.

Eventually she stumbled across the RollerBug website and Rollergirl.ca. More importantly, on the Rollergirl website, she found a web forum devoted to starting roller derby in Canada and discovered that there were discussions ongoing in Toronto, Hamilton, Edmonton and Vancouver, and then she saw that lone post about Montreal.

Kwasny, now officially Tush, ran with that MissTheMeaner post, starting a MySpace page and checking out roller rinks. Eventually, after getting enough traffic on the site, she organized a meeting at Foufounes Electriques, one of the city's most venerable underground music venues. Fourteen people came to the initial meeting. "The original people who showed up were all from different backgrounds and scenes. I thought we were to get one type of person, but it ended up being pretty random," she says of that first meeting. While it may have been mostly random, the first person through the door was someone Tush knew from the music scene, Marie-Chantal Trachy, the women who would come to be known as Trash 'n' Smash, another key figure in the early days of the revival in Canada.

In a 2007 interview in Montreal's indie weekly, *Mirror*, Kwasny tried to explain roller derby: "The new era of roller derby is a mix of burlesque and competitive sport and rock 'n' roll – that's what's cool about it. It's a sport, but it's slightly off" (quoted in Zanin). This seems to sum up that first generation of Canadian women playing roller derby and their attitude toward it: sure it's a sport, "but it's slightly off." Not that it wasn't athletic – it is a contact sport played at high speeds on quad roller skaters after all. And Tush herself, despite her early-twenties focus on the music scene and partying, had a fairly extensive athletic background. The daughter of competitive athletes herself (her mother was a national-level competitive swimmer), Tush had grown up playing a variety of sports, including hockey.

It's extraordinary how similar all of these early stories are, from the rock 'n' roll influence, to the falling in love with images online, right down the to the initial meetings in bars. And in another striking similarity with Toronto, the Montreal skaters also had to look outward to the suburbs to find a place to skate, eventually coming across Laval's La Récréathèque as their early training venue. And to further show the ties between the rock scene and early Canadian flat track roller derby, Montreal's first coach, Dom Castelli, was a prominent promoter in the city's music scene.

Although Tush had initially started Montreal Roller Derby as a single-team league in April 2006, by August and their trip to Toronto for the D-Day tournament, they had enough skaters to form two teams. Within a year, by the time Montreal opened its doors to the public for its first house league season, the league was already divided into its three home teams.

3. Edmonton
While there was definite early verbal contact, especially through Rollergirl.ca's Skate Forum, the earliest Eastern and Western

Canadian roller derby leagues sprouted up in relative isolation from each other until about 2009. In Edmonton, late in 2005, Sherry Bontkes – inspired by the rising flat track revival happening in the States – decided to fulfill her lifelong dream of becoming a roller girl.

In an interview with the *Edmonton Journal* in March 2006, Bontkes, already known by her derby name Sour Cherry, admits that as a child she used to love watching the wild and raucous roller derby and Roller Games of the '70s and told the *Journal* that she had "wanted to do it since [she] was like eight years old" ("Local Oil City Rollers Hoping for a Roller Derby Renaissance"). By February of the following year, as a direct result of the influence of the *Rollergirls* debut on A&E, Sour Cherry had managed to recruit fourteen skaters. Similar to the leagues starting up in Eastern Canada, the draw was more the attitude and the reputation than the sport itself, and early conflicts about the direction of the revival are evident in interviews from that time. Sour Cherry initially envisioned a version of the sport closer to the Roller Games of the mid '70s and '80s, and the carnivalized version that was presented on the *Rollergirls* TV show. For example, in the early years of the revival, it was common for leagues to have a penalty wheel that skaters who made an infraction would have the option to spin to determine their penalty instead of serving it in the penalty box. Some of Sour Cherry's early ideas were to make skaters mud wrestle, jello fight or endure "spank alley," a popular punishment held over from the earliest days in Austin that saw a skater circle the track bent over while fans who surrounded it spanked her ("Local Oil City Rollers").

One of the first Oil City skaters, Lethal Strawberry, saw past the gimmicks right away. "Sure, it's a show and there's a lot of showmanship," she admitted to the *Edmonton Journal* in that introductory 2006 article, "but it's definitely not fake ... It has to be a sport," she wisely concluded. "There are serious athletes out there."

The penalty wheel never caught on in Edmonton, nor anywhere else in Canada, and it had mostly been eliminated in the US by 2006 as well in favour of the more athletically minded penalty box. Although playfully, Oil City was known for their penalty couches (two loveseats located in the centre of the track).

While the league would be up and running with two house league teams by 2007 (the Dirty Derby Dolls and the Kryptkeepers – as with Hammer City, these wouldn't necessarily be the same teams who moved forward with the league), perhaps the most important moment in Oil City's early history and one of the defining moments of the early Canadian revival came in December 2006.

For eight years, from 2006 to 2014, Oil City played in what was one of the legendary venues in Canadian derby, a venue they affectionately called The Grindhouse, officially known as Xtreme Sports Roller Hockey in 2006, and then Metro Sportsplex until its shuttering in the summer of 2014. It was here where the first-ever cross-border women's flat track roller derby game was played. Two years before Canadian leagues began to develop travel, or all-star, teams, Oil City provided the precursor to that movement when they faced off against Denver's legendary Rocky Mountain Rollergirls, one of the founding leagues of the WFTDA. Oil City lost by what at the time was a massive blowout, 110–34, but more importantly, roller derby in Western Canada had been born.

While the Smoke City Betties' August 2006 D-Day tournament brought together the earliest Eastern Canadian teams, in July of 2007, Oil City hosted their early Western counterpart,

Vancouver's Terminal City Rollergirls, at the Grindhouse. Terminal City would take the win, 108–85, kicking off competitive roller derby in Canada's West. The Edmonton hosts would be surprised by Vancouver, citing their opponent's speed as being the most impressive aspect of their game. On the league's blog, Oil City would write about the "amazing jamming" of one of the Terminal City skaters who went by the simple name RollerGirl ("Sour Cherry").

4. Vancouver

While the online presence of American leagues, the rise of social networking sites like MySpace and the debut of *Rollergirls* all had a direct impact on the development of the game in Canada, perhaps the single most important tool in the development of early Canadian roller derby was the Skate Forum of Lisa Suggitt's Rollergirl.ca website.

Suggitt, who started skating at four years old, was known as RollerGirl long before she ever stepped foot on a roller derby track, at least as far back as 2001 when the sport was just beginning to lift off in the States. Gaining a reputation as an "aggressive roller skater" (Zimmerman), a style of skating that was also know as vert – vertical – skating, in the skate park and bowls in and around Vancouver, but unable to find adequate skates to comfortably pursue her vert-skating interest, Suggitt ended up building her own, using hockey boots and skateboard wheels and trucks. This led to experimenting with other boots such as combat boots and low-cut sneakers. As with Kandy Barr in Toronto, RollerGirl was unknowingly verging on making the kind of roller skates that would come to be used in roller derby. By summer 2002 she was selling customized skates (Mackin), by March of 2003 she had her website up and running and her mission, as reported by Kate Zimmerman in a *National Post* interview in 2003, was "to spread the word about roller skating in general, and aggressive roller skating in particular." By the fall of 2003, Suggitt was also giving lessons at a suburban roller skating rink in Surrey, hoping to put together a team of female aggressive skaters. At that time, the sport of roller derby was far from her thoughts.

Roller derby actually has deep, historic roots in British Columbia, being born first as an intramural sport at the University of British Columbia in the 1940s ("Jokers Staging Intramural Skating Derby Tomorrow"). Started by a, from all accounts, "wild" unofficial fraternity called the Jokers, they borrowed the coed, endurance format of the sport that was being popularized by Leo Seltzer in the States in the late '30s and early '40s. The intramural league lasted three seasons from 1946 to 1947. While apparently popular at the time, after the folding of the intramural league, it would take five decades for the competitive version of the sport to return.

Fast-forward three years from the launch of RollerGirl's website in 2003 to January 2006. Michelle Lamoureux, soon to be known as Micki Mercury, caught the debut of *Rollergirls*. Almost immediately Micki placed an ad on Craigslist about potential interest in starting a roller derby league in Vancouver. Within a month a few dozen girls had responded and the first public meeting was held at Suzanne Gardiner's house (a.k.a. Trixi Trippin Chix). It wasn't long after that when Vancouver's first roller derby league was branded the Terminal City Rollergirls.

Despite her RollerGirl nickname, Suggitt was initially skeptical about derby. "They were wearing fishnets and tutus and they couldn't skate," she admits was her first impression (personal interview). But a broken tailbone and concussion pushed her away from aggressive skating to the, ironically, safer sport of roller derby, and given her extensive skating background, she took on a key role with the training committee in those early days.

Within a year, on May 5, 2007, Terminal City opened the doors to the public, playing a game featuring two unnamed teams branded by colours, the Red Rollitas and the Black Bandidas, a trend that continued through the first season as teams such as Red Rollers and Black-Eyed Betties would compete. By the time the second season began in April 2008, the league had divided into three distinct house league teams. As with Hammer City's Steel Town Tank Girls, the names of the first teams would show their roots in the rock 'n' roll scene with the Faster Pussycats – which also harkens back to the classic Russ Meyer exploitation film about a bunch of tough women on a violent road trip – but also directly to its third-wave roots with a direct reference to the riot grrrl movement with the Riot Girls.

The Terminal City All-Stars would also debut in 2007, when the team travelled to Edmonton to play Oil City in that first Western Canadian inter-league game. The formation of Terminal City gave Canada its first five leagues, and completed the foundation on which the rest of the country's community could grow.

★ ★ ★

When you walk into a roller derby venue for a game, you will be greeted by roller girls at the door who will take your ticket, you will buy merch from skaters working vendor booths, you will see skaters preparing the track, working cameras, serving beer, directing traffic. Every aspect of your experience will have been designed, built and executed by the very skaters you have gone to see on the track.

This DIY ethos extends well beyond the game-day experience. Roller derby in Canada is a sport completely built by the skaters for the skaters and it's no different anywhere else that flat track roller derby has developed either. On their feet, they wear skates designed and sometimes even made by skaters (RollerGirl, My Roll Life, Antik – all skater-owned skate companies), their uniforms come from companies owned by skaters (Pivotstar, Monster Muffin), even the arm bands that are wrapped around the skaters' upper arms to display their numbers were made by skaters for a skater-owned endeavour (Sugarbomb). Three of the key early members of the first five leagues of Canadian roller derby exemplify this DIY mission: RollerGirl (RollerGirl), Kandy Barr (RollerBug) and Georgia W. Tush (who eventually founded the company Neon Skates) were not only early founding members of their respective leagues, directly in Tush's case, but were involved in the production and distribution of the products necessary for the game. All started distribution companies and all eventually opened brick-and-mortar outlets in their respective cities. All helped build a sport from nothing.

The women who were drawn early on to the flat track roller derby movement were often drawn by the sense of community they felt: it was welcoming, it was enlightening, it was liberating and, most of all, it was empowering. But if that was what brought them to the game, it was the DIY nature of the sport that hooked them. To be a roller derby player, especially in the early part of the revival, was to invest your life into not only developing a game, but also in developing the infrastructure to support it. The majority of the leagues currently operating are not-for-profits, while some are built on a co-op style or shareholder business model, but in any model the leaders of the leagues – from the elected boards that run the leagues to the treasurers that handle the money to the people who build the websites – are uniformly skaters. This holds true for the smallest rec-style league in small-town Ontario to the executive in charge of the Women's Flat Track Derby Association.

Even the WFTDA itself is built on a membership-owned model, where every league that plays under the banner, from the most competitive Division 1 teams right down to the least competitive, are equal members and get an equal vote in everything from the association's competitive rankings and playoff model to the most minute rules updates. While this has led to complaints that change often occurs too slowly, it has ensured that skaters own their own sport and the image of it that is presented. University of Alabama sociologist Nancy J. Finley has written about this importance of ownership in the music scenes and how, in the riot grrrl movement, the DIY philosophy allowed women to control their images and they resisted dominance this way (366). And it's not just the women who play either; even I was quickly swept up in the game's machine, first in writing, then in broadcasting. I even spent a few seasons behind the benches of Toronto's travel teams: once you get interested, it's nearly impossible not to get involved.

It could be argued that although it was the DIY ethos that kept roller derby a little punk rock in the early going, the spectacle was heightened and played with ironically as evidenced by team and skater names. While there was a certain tension playing out in all the early leagues between the sport or spectacle direction, it is, arguably, the DIY aspect that has pushed the sport more toward the mainstream, at least in terms of competitiveness. The DIY focus causes skaters to invest so much into it that they want something to be proud of; they have fallen in love with the sport. This prevailing attitude is what eventually pushed the skaters toward pursuing roller derby not simply as a lifestyle, but as an athletic endeavour, despite the fact that many of them had backgrounds far removed from athletics. From barrooms and punk rock shows to boardrooms and sports arenas, the DIY ethos drove the participants to not only develop the game of roller derby, but to build it in their own various images.

nerding out

FIVE THINGS YOU NEED TO KNOW ABOUT THE MODERN ROLLER DERBY REVIVAL

Before diving much deeper into how the evolution of the modern game fits into the history of roller derby, for those uninitiated into the sport and maybe even a refresher for those who are, there are a few key things about the revival that you need to know.

1. The revival was started by women

This might seem obvious to some, but it is an incredibly important distinction to make. The modern revival of roller derby is so tied to women that many people have the false memory that the sport was always played primarily by women, which is not true. Since Leo Seltzer first began to refine the sport in the 1930s and through its various incarnations until 2000, the sport was always coed, generally alternating between men's and women's lines on the track. However, the revival has redefined roller derby as a women's sport that also happens to be played by men. It is a major distinction to make and one that is at the philosophical heart of the game.

From the initial stirrings in 2001, women defined the parameters of the sport: they defined the way it was played, they created the community that would support it and they built the infrastructure roller derby needed to function. Although there are echoes of mainstream influence in the organizational structures, the creation and governing of flat track roller derby is unprecedented in sports history. It eschewed traditional sports models in favour of figuring it out on its own. Mainstream sports is a male-dominated arena; those initial roller girls, who often had no formal sports background, had zero interest in pursuing those traditional frameworks and have infused the game with a strong feminist underpinning. This is such an important aspect of the revival that many skaters feel uncomfortable about men skating, and some skaters even choose to ignore roller derby's deep roots in the twentieth century and are sometimes reluctant to acknowledge the influence of previous incarnations of the game.

2. The game is played on a flat track

This is mostly true. The primary surface upon which the modern revival of roller derby is played is a flat one.

Most people, if they remember it at all, know roller derby either from the last televised run of the sport, in the '60s and early '70s, or through the various attempts to bring back the televised version of the game in the late '70s, '80s and late '90s. In all of these cases, the game was played on a banked track.

The modern revival, beginning in Austin in 2001, also initially envisioned a banked track version of the game. But by 2003, a group of skaters had committed to playing the game on a flat surface, as they didn't have the money to purchase or build a banked track and then also pay to house it. One of those initial "flat trackers," Melissa Joulwan, in her early book on the revival,

Rollergirl, described the process of creating the flat track as figuring out what the banked track would look like if it were "smashed flat" (55). With the aid of a CAD program the somewhat awkward dimensions were hashed out. Contrary to another popular perception, the track is not round or an oval but a slightly modified ellipse. The track is about fifty-five feet (seventeen metres) across and eighty-eight feet (twenty-seven metres) long, slightly wider on the outside turns (turns 2 and 4) to account for speed gained on the two straightaways. Slightly raised (usually rope) taped-down borders mark the inner and outer boundaries.

Banked track roller derby does exist in the revival and has been slowly gaining momentum for as long as the revival has been going on, but its growth has been slowed by the cost. Currently, the dominant banked track rule sets are the Roller Derby Coalition of Leagues (RDCL) played primarily on the west coast of the United States, and the Modern Athletic Derby Endeavor (MADE), which is primarily played in the US's Northeast and in the eastern Midwest as well.

3. It's real

There is a misconception that roller derby was traditionally fake, which isn't exactly true. While roller derby has skirted the sports entertainment business since its first days, it wasn't until later that the sport veered fully and completely into that territory.

Leo Seltzer had always envisioned roller derby as a legitimate sport and even entertained visions of its inclusion in the Olympics. When Leo's son, Jerry, took over the game he continued his father's expansion of the sport into an actual national league, mirroring the professional sports at the time. But while he maintained control over the locations, names and even rosters of the teams, he let the skaters do their own thing on the track

(Coppage, 42). While stacked rosters could influence who the dominant teams were, the only fake aspect of roller derby from 1949 to 1973 were some pro-wrestling-like trips, elbows and staged fights that almost always happened between jams and rarely affected gameplay. It wasn't until the late '70s through to the '90s when the post-Seltzer television incarnations were the only thing going that the "sport" became a full on entertainment spectacle with virtually everything being staged and manipulated for the audience.

During the earliest days of the twenty-first century revival, there was some uncertainty about how authentic the game would be, but by 2003 the earliest skaters of the revival were already well on their way to treating roller derby purely as a legitimate sport. Rules were written and have been refined to that end since. By 2006, the existing teams played in a national championship that continues to be the goal of the vast majority of the flat track teams today. While any roller derby league is free to play the game however they see fit, teams that compete in the WFTDA's competitive divisions must adhere to a strict sanctioning protocol that guarantees equal competitive ground and maintains the legitimacy of the games.

4. There are three positions

Every player in roller derby plays at least one of three positions: blocker, pivot or jammer. Sometimes, multi-talented skaters play all three roles on the track over the course of a game, but for the most part, players are designated their positions based on particular skill sets.

The teams consist of fourteen players with five players (each) on the track at a time. At the beginning of a game, four skaters from each team, called the pack, line up anywhere they like in the starting area. This is a thirty-foot-long (twenty-seven-metre-long) piece of track on a straightaway between two lines called the jammer line and the pivot line. Three of these four pack skaters are called blockers, and their helmets are bare. The fourth skater in the pack, the pivot, wears a single thick stripe along the centre of her helmet. The pivot stripe is not painted directly on the helmet, but is instead on a removable helmet cover, sometimes called a panty, that resembles a swimming cap.

Lining up behind the jammer line, and therefore behind the pack, is the jammer. The jammer is indicated by a helmet cover with stars on each side. The jammer is generally a fast and agile skater, as it is her job to burst through the pack and eventually lap the opposing blockers to score points.

Traditionally, the pivot was a leadership role on the track, often stationed at the front of the pack to control play. But the pivot also acts as a backup jammer if, for example, a team's designated jammer is beaten into exhaustion by the opposition. In flat track roller derby, the jammer must remove her helmet cover, the star, from her helmet and pass it directly to the pivot, who then must put the cover on her helmet over top of the stripe to become the new jammer. This is called a star pass and once the pivot has become the jammer, there is no passing the cover back.

5. Most points wins!

The majority of flat track players, and virtually everyone outside of the US, plays under the WFTDA rule set, but regardless of the rule set, in all forms of roller derby, the team with the most points at the end of the game wins.

One of the great and fascinating aspects of the game is the necessity to play both offence and defence simultaneously, as, barring penalties, both teams have a jammer on the track at any given time. Although there are a number of ways a jam can go, a standard flat track roller derby jam would see one team gaining lead jammer status, scoring four points, one for each opposing blocker and pivot legally passed, and then calling it off quickly before the opposing jammer is able to complete a pass of her own, ending the jam 4–0.

The game is played in two thirty-minute halves. Each half is broken up by a series of two-minute jams that can end early if a specially designated skater, the lead jammer, decides to end it by tapping her hips.

A whistle begins each jam. Ideally, seven on-skate referees will call the game, policing illegal actions with penalties very similar to those in hockey: no tripping, elbowing, hitting from behind, et cetera, while also ensuring that the pack is maintained. The blockers and pivot must follow strict rules governing the formation of the pack so as to avoid the breakout of a race, where skaters simply chase each other around the track; blockers are only able to engage each other or the jammers when a proper pack is formed. Penalties are thirty seconds long, and if one team's jammer incurs a penalty, that team is incapable of scoring until the jammer returns to the track.

The first lap of a jam is a race between the two jammers, with the jammer who is first able to legally get through the pack being declared lead jammer. On the second pass, or lap, both jammers are eligible to score. The only advantage the lead jammer has is the ability to end the jam when she wants by twice tapping her hips with her hands. This ends the jam, whereby both teams have thirty seconds to reset their lines and put a new jammer on the track.

Barring a tie game, in which a single sudden-death jam is played, the team with the most points at the conclusion of the second half wins.

riot grrrls on wheels

THE HISTORY OF THE ROLLER DERBY REVIVAL AND THE BIRTH OF FLAT TRACK ROLLER DERBY (2001–2006)

During the last weekend of April 2009, I attended the second-ever Beast of the East tournament in Montreal. Designed as a double-elimination tournament featuring the top sixteen house league teams in Eastern Canada, in 2009, for the first time, there actually were sixteen Canadian teams available. During the first tournament in 2008, one of the home teams from Buffalo's Queen City Roller Girls, the Devil Dollies, took part to fill out the bracket, but in 2009 the teams were all representing leagues in Ontario and Quebec.[1]

Originally conceived as a continuation of the Betties' D-Day tournament, the importance of the Beast of the East has grown over time. It has become an annual celebration of the sport, a reunion for some of the oldest leagues in the Canadian game and those involved in it. It's also an opportunity for less-experienced skaters to play in a weekend-long competitive tournament. House league or home teams are often overlooked in terms of competition, but they remain the top developmental opportunity for the future skaters of the competitive all-star or travel teams.

Because the tournament does not feature those ultra-competitive travel teams, the attitude around the two-day event is also noticeably lighter.

Since most Canadian roller derby seasons begin when ice is removed from rinks, the timing of the tournament in the last weekend of April means that for many skaters from Quebec and Ontario the Beast is the first chance they have to play in a competitive game in any season or even in their careers for rookies.

In 2009, less than two years after discovering the sport, my partner made her skating debut at the Beast. We'd moved from Montreal to Toronto and Jan had become a blocker for The Death Track Dolls. It was terrifying for both of us, but I admit it was probably more so for me. To add to it all, the luck of the draw had placed Jan's team up against one of the pre-tournament favourites and one of the first teams we'd ever seen play: Les Filles du Roi (or FDR).

I was sitting in my old spot at turn 1 of the suicide seats when Jan, now Downright Dirty Dawson (eventually just Dawson), lined up as a blocker against FDR jammer Beater Pan-Tease, a woman who only a year before had guided Jan through her first tentative steps on quads. Dawson stared hard at her – wide-eyed – the adrenaline flowing as she waited to experience the game for the first time, probably wondering what it was going to feel like – real contact from real opponents – and juiced on that anticipation. Beater winked, all her experience showing in her calmness, and when the whistle blew, she burst through the pack easily to become the lead jammer. Despite the short nature of the game – the games at the Beast are only twenty minutes long – FDR crushed the Dolls 77–6, but it was one of my favourite games of roller derby ever. I may have shed a tear or two that game.

However, in terms of the bigger picture, Dawson's first game would not be the most life-altering thing that would happen to me during that tournament.

I was still getting used to the derby scene at that point and was thrilled to have an opportunity to see the teams from Hammer City, whose Harlots had won the inaugural tournament in '08, though sadly the Tank Girls hadn't survived, and at this point were replaced by the Death Row Dames. Also in attendance were the Forest City Derby Girls, from London, Ontario, who had played in the 2008 edition as well; Tri-City Roller Girls, from Kitchener-Waterloo, who eventually became Tri-City Roller Derby; Ottawa Roller Derby and Rideau Valley Roller Girls (I didn't know at the time that the two Ottawa-based leagues were going through a somewhat acrimonious split); and, of course, the hosts, Montreal, who would dominate that year. There was also a second team from Toronto, the GTA Rollergirls, a league led by a husband and wife duo. The two had originally been on the Smoke City Betties but left during the continental shift that had occurred in Toronto's derby scene during the formation of ToRD in fall 2006. While I was beginning to recognize teams and even player names from other cities, I was just getting to know the referees, and there was one referee whom I definitely didn't recognize.

He was a slim man, with ultra-thin calves covered by black knee-high socks. Nerdy, with wire-rimmed glasses, he wore the standard referee zebra stripes, but the top flared out at the bottom into a pleated black skirt. I also noticed that when he wasn't refereeing, he was dutifully typing away on a laptop. I'd learn later that he went by the name Justice Feelgood Marshall and was, among a variety of other roles in the sport, the chief writer and editor for a website called the Derby News Network (DNN). When I went back to Toronto at the end of the weekend and looked up derbynewsnetwork.com for the first time, I was astonished to see that he had published a game-by-game, blow-by-blow, traditional sports recap of the complete tournament. It would be the first time that I would read about flat track roller derby just as I would read about any other sport, as opposed to some "such-in-such by day, derby doll by night" fluff piece in the lifestyle section of a newspaper. It was profoundly altering for me as a fan not only of flat track roller derby, but as a fan of sports, and, perhaps most important of all, as a writer.

In the spring of 2009, I was still only vaguely aware of the larger roller derby community, but DNN gave me the opportunity to learn about it, so I dived into its archives with ferocity. Since Montreal and Toronto had created all-star teams to compete against Hammer City in 2008, there had been talk of Hammer City and Montreal looking to officially join the, then exclusively American, governing body of the game, WFTDA. Through the Derby News Network I learned of the competitive regions that the WFTDA had created and the playoff system that it was still building. I read about the 2008 playoffs and thrilling national tournament, the third WFTDA championship. I learned that in 2009 the association had divided into four regions for the first time to accommodate the uniformly accelerated growth of the sport. I learned about the first generation of stars of the game and the top teams who, at the time, were the Texas Rollergirls (Austin), Tucson Roller Derby, Gotham Girls Roller Derby (New York), the Kansas City Roller Warriors and Seattle's Rat City Rollergirls. I also learned that after experimenting with a live video stream accompanied by a play-by-play text-based webcast in 2008, that DNN was going to attempt to live stream the 2009 WFTDA Nationals, complete with colour commentary.

Suddenly, the larger world of flat track roller derby opened up to me. One question entered my mind, inexplicably, for the first time: How did this all happen? Where had this sport come from? I made it my goal to find out. Given that the complete renaissance of the sport had been in the twenty-first century alongside the rise of social media, the answers proved surprisingly simple to find.

From DNN I found links to other sites like Derby Tron and Flat Track Stats, an independent website that had created a complex algorithm to rank teams. Beyond these websites I managed to grab a copy of Mel Joulwan's book *Rollergirl* and saw the film *Hell on Wheels*, directed by Bob Ray. Both are essential documents in understanding the deepest roots of the flat track revival. Using these resources, I was able to work backwards in time, through Gotham's WFTDA Championship win in 2008 on to Kansas City's championship run in 2007 and finally back to the 2006 Dust Devil Invitational and what is now known as the first ever WFTDA Championship, won, naturally, by Austin's Texecutioners: the women who had quite literally written the rules of the sport.

It's rare to see the birth of a game. To see that precise moment where an idea, a philosophy or the beginning of a movement shifts into something concrete. In hockey, there are numerous frozen ponds across Eastern Canada that lay claim to being the watering hole that finally gave birth to the game, with Windsor, Nova Scotia – near my hometown of Kentville – generally considered to be the place where the great-white version of Irish hurley on ice shifted to become a new game entirely. But that is up for debate and it may be that sports cannot possibly be traced back to their evolutionary starting points.

And while the origin of roller derby as a game played on quad skates within the confines of a restricted oval is equally murky, with references dating as far back as the late nineteenth century, there is no question at all about the birth of the modern, flat track version of the game played primarily by women. Roller derby, which had officially been left for dead in 2000 with the demise of TNN's flashy attempt at a sports-entertainment revival called *RollerJam*, had been reborn in Austin, Texas, in 2001, shortly after a group of women were brought together by a shady figure who went by the name Devil Dan. Dan had the vague idea of re-establishing the sport of roller derby as a form of performance art closer to the entertainment spectacles of the '80s and '90s revivals than the Seltzer sport of the '50s, '60s and '70s (Atwell, 39). While he managed to inspire the women to revive roller derby, his vision for the game, and his place within it, did not last long.

In a stroke of profound luck, the earliest days of the revival were all caught on camera. Just by chance, filmmakers Bob Ray and Werner Campbell were looking for a documentary subject in Austin, their expected subject having fallen through, and they stumbled upon the first women involved in the revival. This began a four-year journey following the genesis of modern roller derby that would result in the incredibly important 2007 film *Hell on Wheels*. The film provides a rare glimpse into the birth of a movement and the early growth of a sport.

From 2001 to 2003, the roller derby revival had been led by Bad Girl Good Women Productions and its quartet of self-proclaimed She-E-Os, who owned the league and made the decisions around its functioning. Dedicated to reviving the banked tracked version of the sport, they played a few campy flat track bouts to try to raise funds to build their track, but spent most of their time recruiting women, fostering a riot grrrl attitude, and trying to gain traction on their idea. They did go as far as to create four teams and decided that everyone involved would take on stage or derby names.

In the spring of 2003, after some major missteps led to some skaters becoming increasingly dissatisfied with the tight-fisted control maintained by the She-E-Os (Barbee and Cohen, 46), a few of the women had an idea of creating a shared-ownership league, where all of the women would have equal say. Eventually, the tension over the direction of the organization led to a crisis that brought nearly all eighty of the skaters together for a meeting held around a campfire in a backyard in Austin. At the meeting, the group of skaters pushing for change gave an ultimatum on shared ownership to the four leaders. The She-E-Os, however, would not relent, and when this became obvious to those in attendance, three quarters of the skaters stood up and walked away from the corporate model laid out by BGGW Productions.

It's a pivotal moment in the documentary, and also a strange moment as the women who had been the protagonists in the story – the She-E-Os – suddenly become the antagonists, and the viewer's loyalties awkwardly shift. Mel Joulwan was one of the outspoken women at the meeting that night, and would tell her side of the story in *Rollergirl*. Mel and the other sixty-five skaters who stood up and walked away from the fire would not abandon the sport and the community they'd all grown to love, but instead, they would collectively form the Texas Rollergirls (TXRG). This would become a DIY, committee-run, skater-owned-and-operated organization comprised of four house league teams and, eventually, a travelling team of all-stars called the Toxecutioners. It was both a practical and philosophical model that would, in a very short period of time, guide the formation of leagues all across the United States: but also a women's movement and a sport, the rapid growth of which would baffle sociologists and sports fans. While the shared ownership model and the DIY ethos behind it would have a huge influence on the sport's popularity, it would be the decision on the playing surface that would truly allow for the massive growth of the game.

Although modern roller derby's Great Divide initially had nothing to do with the way the sport was played on the track, the philosophical differences that had led to the split would be reflected in the changes that would go into creating the new roller derby. Primarily, while BGGW continued to work toward becoming an old-school banked track league, eventually changing its name to the TXRD Lonestar Rollergirls, the newly formed Texas Rollergirls decided to give up on the idea of a banked track and rewrote the rules to play the game on a flat surface. Although not obvious at the time, this created a dramatic shift in the way the sport could and had to be played. The lowering of the track democratized the game and set the stage for a grassroots explosion.

Before the Texas Rollergirls, one of the challenges that the banked track sport had always faced was that it was inaccessible. The fact that roller derby required such a unique, and expensive, playing surface meant that there had never been a grassroots movement of amateur players who had grown up around the sport; the game had never spread beyond the players people saw on their TV screens. In all its previous incarnations, roller derby had, essentially, been a single league with central ownership that travelled the country and remained a once-or-twice-a-year event to be watched passively. There were no local leagues, no one ever played or even got to watch it live on a regular-enough basis to understand the rules with any clarity. As a spectacle, banked track roller derby favoured speed over strategy, drama over competition. The banked track easily became a platform for the kind of staged sports entertainment that typified the final stages of the Seltzer-run banked track roller derby in the early '70s and became the central aspect of all of the attempted revivals in the '70s, '80s and '90s. Which is, in part, why the Lonestar Rollergirls were so appealing to A&E and why it was *that* league, the banked track one and not the less flashy TXRG flat trackers, that was eventually chronicled on the mainstream television program *Rollergirls* in 2006.

But it was the story of that split, and the decisions leading up to it, that not only formed the early mythology of the revival of the game, but also laid out the literal and philosophical structures that would govern its rise. The Texas Rollergirls' league structure – house league teams feeding a travel team – would be mimicked and copied. Run by an elected board of skaters, the league functioned through a series of skater-run committees and was committed to the self-ownership model that the banked trackers had initially been opposed to. This too would become the organizational model of nearly every flat track league in the world. The focus of the new league was clearly built on a DIY approach, from the infrastructure of the league right down to the flat track marked with duct tape.

On April 27, 2003, at the Playland Skate Center in Austin, Texas, two of the Texas Rollergirls house league teams, the Hotrod Honeys and the Honky Tonk Heartbreakers, played the first official game of flat track roller derby. Very soon after, the flat track revolution would begin, and once it got started, it moved quickly. Nearly simultaneously, Arizona Roller Derby sprung up in Phoenix, followed by an offshoot in Tucson. In November 2004 the Texas Rollergirls and Tucson Roller Derby played the first travel team game featuring all-star lineups representing each league

(Joulwan, 231). As TXRG shared its rules and organizational experience, other leagues quickly followed. In 2004 leagues started in cities across the US: in New York, with Gotham Girls Roller Derby; Seattle, Rat City Rollergirls; Raleigh, Carolina Rollergirls; Minneapolis-St. Paul, Minnesota RollerGirls; Madison, Wisconsin, Mad Rollin' Dolls; Kansas City, Kansas City Roller Warriors; and in Portland, with the Rose City Rollers. Once word started getting out and the media slowly started to catch on, the growth became expansive (Joulwan, 240; Barbee and Cohen, 52).

In 2005 the original twenty flat track organizations formed the United Leagues Coalition (ULC) (Joulwan, 241). Along with representatives from the original 2004 wave, skaters representing Dallas; Atlanta; Providence, Rhode Island; Boston; Huntsville, Alabama; Chicago and New Orleans rounded out the coalition. In August 2005, the ULC held its first conference in Chicago, which also happened to be the birthplace of the original Seltzer roller derby. At this conference the rules and practicalities were standardized, and the idea of a national tournament featuring all-star travel teams was formed. But most importantly, the guiding philosophy of "by the skaters, for the skaters" was born. By the end of 2005, the first officially sanctioned flat track roller derby rules would be released, and the ULC would be rebranded as the Women's Flat Track Derby Association, the governing body for the roughly thirty-five flat track leagues that existed at the time and still the dominant governing body of the sport today (Joulwan, 242; Barbee and Cohen, 62).

With the stage so well set, the flat track revolution would truly begin in early 2006.

By February, the first few episodes of *Rollergirls* had aired, and women across North America were starting to get inspired.

However, the dominant story in the quietly growing media storm was not about the TXRD Lonestar Rollergirls and their banked track league, but the first-ever national championship flat track tournament, the Dust Devil Invitational.

On the weekend of February 24–26 in Tucson, Arizona, the founding leagues of flat track roller derby skated in the first-ever multi-team roller derby tournament. Not surprisingly, Austin's Texas Rollergirls defeated Tucson Roller Derby 129–96 in the final to win the inaugural WFTDA Championship, but more importantly, the national press had taken just enough notice to spread the word (Joulwan, 261). The sport would never be the same.

By the end of 2006, flat track roller derby, born only three years before in Austin, was played in six countries and consisted of around one hundred fifty leagues. It was an astonishing rate of growth that would continue in the following years.

By the time I was discovering all of this in 2009, the sport was a thriving, increasingly popular and global game. I recognized the direct influence of those early flat trackers on all the skaters I saw at the Beast of the East in the feminism; the rigid, nearly religious, adherence to the DIY ethic; and, of course, the passion for the game.

That fall the Derby News Network broadcast the 2009 WFTDA playoffs and I was glued to my computer screen, enthralled by the colour commentary, by the traditional athletic narrative that was being laid out before me.

I continued to follow DNN closely, checking in almost daily, until its eventual demise in fall 2014. But at the beginning of 2009 as the history of the sport bubbled up around me, I began to think that maybe writing about roller derby was something I could do, as no one was writing about it with any regularity at the time in Canada. While there were colourful, wonderful trackside announcers who seemed integrated into the spectacle, and therefore beyond what I was capable of, hearing that DNN web-streamed broadcast got me thinking that maybe there was a place for me to talk about the game as well.

By the end of 2009, I was as devoted to and wrapped up in the game as most skaters, and I'd been branded with my own derby name, the Derby Nerd. I was ready to get involved.

eight-wheeled freedom

ROLLER DERBY AS A REFLECTION
OF ITS ERA (1880 – 2000)

In the twentieth century history of roller derby, two names in particular stand out; Joanie "Blonde Bomber" Weston and Gwen "Skinny Minnie" Miller. Weston, a tall, athletic, striking blond, was often referred to as the "Golden Girl" (Mabe, 51), while Miller was the undersized underdog, the crafty, jukey skater who used her speed and agility to fake out her opponents, which allowed her to excel despite her limited size. They were crowd favourites, women who were the faces of the game during its peak popularity in the 1960s and '70s, and their names are still often invoked today when people are reminded of the sport.

Yet if you ask most modern roller girls who they look back to, it's Ann Calvello that many consider to be the spirit mother of the modern game. Calvello played roller derby off and on, in its various incarnations, for a remarkable seven decades, beginning when she debuted in 1948 at the age of eighteen (Mabe, 52). Incredibly athletic, but also flamboyant, she was the woman that the fans loved to hate. Known for her over-the-top tan; her tattoos, which all included lions; her elaborate makeup and wildly dyed hair, she was the villain to Weston's heroine, the "heel" of roller derby (Joulwan, 48). It was Calvello who the Texas Lonestar Roller Derby girls sought out on the television show *Rollergirls* (on which she made a few appearances) and her name adorns TXRD's trophy, the Calvello Cup, which was the first trophy of the contemporary roller derby era and remains the top prize for teams in that house league.

It's easy to see the allure of Calvello for the modern skater. While Weston was the face of roller derby, the representative of the organization and of ownership, Calvello was the rebel. She was the anarchist who pushed back against the ownership, who flipped her middle finger to the mainstream and who faced her opponents with a brutal ferocity. She was known to travel with her own gold chalice that she would force bartenders to fill for her at after-parties (Deford, 30), she hooked up with younger male skaters when on the road (ibid., 55) and, not surprisingly, was the all-time leader in penalty minutes (Coppage, 66). However, she was also the off-track leader of the group and all accounts say that while she had a forceful personality off the track as well as on, she was actually quite friendly and was the skater who kept everyone together (Mabe, 97; Deford, 54). Maybe it's that dichotomy that the modern skater can relate to: having an on-track persona that you can turn off when the final whistle blows and real life resumes. Whatever the appeal, Calvello represented the freedom afforded to women in the sport of roller derby, even in the less-than-equal decades of the '50s and '60s.

Roller derby in particular, and roller skating in general, has provided a space and an outlet for women, although the relationship has had its peaks and valleys. Almost since the moment roller skates were created, a certain kind of woman has been inspired to strap on eight wheels.

Pre-History: 1880 - 1935

The modern roller skate can be traced back to two men: James Plimpton and M. C. Henley. Plimpton invented the strap-on skate in 1863 (Konner, 7), but the shape and style of modern skates can be more clearly seen in a patent that was given in November 1880 to M.C. Henley of Richmond, Indiana (Tate; Storms, 68). The early history of people strapping wheels on their feet is a bit foggier and is generally traced back to Belgium in the 1760s (Zimmerman; Mackin), but it was Henley who patented the elements that still make the modern roller skates. From the trucks that acted as an axle for the wheels, to the cushions between the trucks and the footplate, and eventually even to ball bearings and the "soundless" non-wooden wheels (Schroeder), Henley designed it. Within a decade, roller skating had become a major pastime with rinks (often featuring hard maple floors) in virtually every corner of America (Storms, 69).

The late nineteenth century was a time of great change, in the US in particular. In the wake of the industrial revolution, the expectations for domestic and social life were changing and "modern" gender roles were being redefined with women not given much space in the newly evolving social sphere. These financial and social changes created a middle class, and along with this came the rise of leisure time. Life was easier for some than it had ever been before and communities were engaging in social lives as they hadn't previously. Competitive athletics and various forms of social functions, dances, for example, were becoming popular. Women, however, were discouraged from taking part in any form of athletics or even from developing their bodies physically (Storms, 69).

As Carolyn Storms discusses in her article "'There's No Sorry in Roller Derby': A Feminist Examination of Identity of Women in the Full Contact Sport of Roller Derby," at the time, roller skating had yet to develop much beyond its roots in the dance halls (70) and was therefore viewed as more of a recreational activity than an athletic or competitive one (69). For women, this meant that they were permitted to take part, unlike other sports. And they did so almost immediately.

There are newspaper articles referring not only to women taking part in roller skating, but also about the activity acting as a liberating one for them (ibid., 69) from as far back as 1883 in Chicago. Beyond the social benefits of skating, the roller rinks provided the first real spaces where women could experience their bodies beyond the monotony of housework that also came with middle class; it offered one of the very few ways that women could develop knowledge of their own physical capabilities (70). The power and importance of this at the time can not be overlooked, and a more direct link between roller derby and the eventual rise of first-wave social feminism could be found in the development of roller skating clubs, social spaces for women where they could meet, talk and roller skate (71).

As skating grew in popularity, so did the criticism of it, and, of course, there was a backlash against women's participation. This led to articles like one in the *Chicago Tribune* in 1885 called "Roller Rink Evil" that criticized the ease by which young single men and women could intermingle at roller rinks (ibid., 70). On the east coast, the *New York Times* also ran a series of articles about the dangers of roller skating for women, focusing more on physical injuries than social ills (71). Led by religious groups and spurred on by a few random deaths loosely attributed to roller skating falls, roller skating was considered a threat to both women's health and their virtue (72). There were even great efforts made to link roller skating to a woman's inability to reproduce (73).

It was also early on in the development of the roller skate that the first organized, competitive activities were developed around the new leisure activity. The first roller skating marathon was held in 1885 at the venerable Madison Square Garden (Barbee and Cohen, 11). It was a six-day endurance event with the winner eventually skating over sixteen hundred kilometres. But even these early races faced a backlash when a few participants died, their deaths once again only tenuously linked to the actual skating (12). Nonetheless, these skating races, eventually referred to as derbies, began the progress toward the creation of roller derby as we know it today.

By 1907, women began to take part in the derbies. Soon the Girls' Branch of the Public Schools Athletic League, who by 1913 supported hundreds of women's athletic clubs that catered to upwards of seventeen thousand members (Storms, 74), sponsored a variety of endurance races. Without any sort of centralized leadership, early derbies happened randomly and without much organization, the length and style changing often. It took nearly two decades of gendered racing before women were permitted to share the track with the men, but when they did, they immediately began to steal the show.

The Leo Seltzer Era: 1935–1959

By the time that Leo Seltzer debuted Transcontinental Roller Derby on August 13, 1935, in the Chicago Coliseum, the world was in the midst of the Great Depression (Barbee and Cohen, 13; Joulwan, 46; Mabe, 23). Simple, cheap, long-form entertainment was popular and every sort of marathon imaginable was being trotted out as entertainment. Leo's roller derby was not much different from the roller skating endurance races that had preceded it, and he even briefly tried having the races on a flat track, but that led to skater exhaustion, and he returned to the more expensive banked track (Joulwan, 14). But after copyrighting the name *roller derby* (Deford, 74), Leo did give it structure, the race was fifty-seven thousand laps to roughly mimic the length across the US, and most importantly, he made it coed (Mabe, 23).

Transcontinental Roller Derby was basically a travelling road show made to look like a sports league. During those early days Leo's roller derby would sweep into town, picking up new skaters along the way – like a travelling circus, people would run away with it (Mabe, 25). In every town and city they would stop in, the skaters would be divided into two squads with one group representing the home team and the other playing as a visiting team (Mabe, 25). Often, the visiting team was from New York (Barbee and Cohen, 17). Even if it wasn't a sport in the traditional sense, the competitors were athletic and the competition was honest. It was incredibly popular from the start, beginning a series of peaks and valleys that roller derby would traverse all the way to the end of the twentieth century.

When it came to hiring skaters for the new roller derby, speed was a factor, but Leo also knew that showmanship sold and he kept a keen eye out for proficient skaters with big personalities (Mabe, 25). During that first wave, participants flocked to the sport looking for the financial stability and housing opportunities it offered, but also for the other benefits that Leo provided for the skaters (26).

Recognizing that at the time women were a bigger draw than men, they were paid equally and sometimes even more (Mabe, 27) and the first stars of the sport were women: Ivy King (Storms, 75) and Josephine "Ma" Bogash, who joined roller derby with her son, Billy (Mabe, 27). Ivy King stole all of the initial headlines in

Chicago after debuting. As a former Canadian speed skater, she had the form and technique to outskate everyone, and set many early speed records in the sport (Storms, 75).

Eventually, Leo started having mid-race jams: short, timed sprints between the competitors in which the winner won extra money. These became exciting breaks, but were also fiercely competitive, and unlike the endurance races, they had contact between skaters as they tried to stay in or move to the front to take home the extra prize (Barbee and Cohen, 14; Phillips, 228). Legend has it that at an event in Miami in 1938, it was Leo's friend, the pulp writer Damon Runyon, who noticed the crowd's intense reaction to these jams and the physical jostling that they resulted in. He then helped Leo write the first rules of what would become roller derby, a points-scoring sport as opposed to an endurance one (Joulwan, 46; Barbee and Cohen, 14; Mabe, 31; Deford, 83; Coppage 12).

This transition pushed Transcontinental Roller Derby toward an even bigger audience and Seltzer kept pushing extremes: he would sometimes try three teams on the track at once and his skaters once even took on the Harlem Globetrotters in basketball, playing on the wooden court with their skates on (Barbee and Cohen, 17).

With the competitive sport now developed, the initial star system began to form, largely built around the rivalry between fan-favourite Gerry Murray and the villain Midge "Toughie" Brasuhn (Barbee and Cohen, 19; Mabe, 37; Phillips, 228). As World War II raged, production of roller skates paused from 1941 to 1945 (Storms, 75), but derby continued and Leo pushed the violence during this time to keep the game compelling to a distracted population (76). The increased violence led to increased crowds and by the time the war ended, roller derby was ready for prime time.

At the 69th Regiment Armory in Manhattan on November 29, 1948, CBS, one of the first television networks, broadcast a game between Gerry Murray's New York Chiefs and Toughie Brasuhn's Brooklyn Red Devils (Barbee and Cohen, 20; Mabe, 38; Joulwan, 20; Coppage, 19). As a spectacle, the sport was a perfect fit for the newly developed television, but the organizational infrastructure was still one based on that of a travelling road show. So in coordination with the new TV deal, Leo expanded into a proper sports league. Transcontinental Roller Derby was rebranded as the National Roller Derby League and it featured six teams that played home games out of their actual cities: New York Chiefs and the Brooklyn Red Devils remained and were joined by the Jersey Jolters, Philadelphia Panthers, Chicago Westerners and Washington (DC) Jets (Mabe, 39; Coppage, 20).

The next three years were Leo's most successful; he even quickly switched television stations, moving to ABC for a better deal (Joulwan, 20; Coppage, 23). On the new network, the sport began broadcasting live every week of the year, proving incredibly popular among women, who counted as upwards of sixty-five per cent of the television audience (Phillips, 230). But the importance and popularity of the medium of television rose even quicker than derby's had and roller derby's first foray into TV ended as abruptly as it began, with it pushed off the air in 1952. The rise of televised baseball and the beginnings of the National Football League changed the perception of sport into a spectator commodity performed nearly exclusively by men, and the unique draw that the women of roller derby initially had faded. Leo kept pushing his vision of the sport and the National Roller Derby League even toured Europe, touching down in England, France and Spain in an attempt to reach new audiences (Mabe,

43), but the bright spotlight it had so recently been bathed in was slowly fading.

The postwar '50s was an interesting time for sport in general and American culture specifically. Despite seeing increased freedoms during the war, women's lives were suddenly more controlled and shaped after the war than they had been in the make-do depression previous to it, and women who did not strictly adhere to these new housewife norms were stigmatized (Storms, 77). They were being removed from the public sphere and the jobs that they had been able to do only half a decade before. This reality was true in virtually every aspect of life for women in America except for one: roller derby.

If the invention of roller skating in the late nineteenth century had given first-wave feminists a space to gather and the collaborative strength to begin social change, then roller derby in the '50s and '60s could be seen as a precursor to second-wave feminists. In roller derby, women and men were equal: Their points were valued equally and they shared the track time equally (Storms, 78). The sport also offered the kind of place where athletic women could flourish and be celebrated as opposed to stigmatized and criticized for not being properly feminine; for example, Joanie Weston at 5'10" and one hundred sixty-five pounds seemed suited for nothing less than an athletic life and was a renowned athlete and surfer off the track, as well as an exceptional skater (Joulwan, 50; Deford, 49). This equality was reflected in the live audiences too, which were often split evenly between men and women, a mixed fan demographic not seen in any other sport at the time (Deford, 7).

Yet as a business, the organization was struggling. Off of television and back to being solely a travelling show, Leo Seltzer passed the torch to his son, Jerry, in 1959.

The Jerry Seltzer Era: 1959-1973

Jerry Seltzer took over a game that seemed to have seen its heyday, but he was committed to bringing it back to its former glory; with the Seltzer name attached so indelibly to the game, it was an important personal mission. Jerry and Leo were not the only Seltzers involved in the sport either. Leo's wife, Belle, had helped with administrative tasks early on, while his daughter, Gloria, whose husband was a referee, ran the office (Coppage, 19). Leo's brother Oscar also ran a roller skate manufacturing company, Roller Derby Skate Company, which made the "official" skates of roller derby (Coppage, 21–22).

As the new commissioner of the sport, and tasked with its revival, Jerry's first decision was to shift operations from the east coast to the west. Now centred out of San Francisco and built around the San Francisco Bay Bombers, Jerry quickly expanded to ten teams (Barbee and Cohen, 21) and changed the name of the organization to the International Roller Derby League (Coppage, 43). New stars rose to the front in the '60s. Joanie Weston, who had started in '54 (Joulwan, 50), Margie Laszlo and Ann Calvello took their places at the centre of the sport's star system. On the men's side Charlie O'Connell, long regarded as one of the finest players of the game; the super-agile Mike Gammon, often called the game's best skater in the '60s and early '70s (Coppage, 82); and Ronnie Robinson, son of boxing great Sugar Ray Robinson, led the way.

Most importantly, Jerry brought roller derby back to TV. The television market was changing rapidly in the '60s and roller derby, now broadcast in syndication, was proving incredibly popular, often garnering more viewers than hockey and baseball at its height in the late '60s (Deford, 7). But while Jerry was an excellent businessman, the sport side of things suffered. There were multiple teams, but they were mostly based out of California. On top of that, there was no defined season as the inconsistencies of syndication didn't allow for the drama of a sequential, season-long narrative (Barbee and Cohen, 23). Despite a new home base and a national audience, the sport was still basically a travelling road show.

It was a strange time for sports in America. America's pastime, baseball, was on a downswing, the golden age having come to an end. It was the era of humble, unflashy superstars like Henry "Hank" Aaron who went about setting records in the most blue-collar, mundane way possible: through quiet, restrained consistency and longevity. Football had yet to fully grasp America by the throat and throttle the country for all it was worth; for example, it was still as lucrative for college graduates to come north and play in the Canadian Football League as it was for them to remain down south and play in the National Football League. But what did thrive in the sports landscape of the 1970s was violence.

While the traditional American pastoral sports were taking a back seat for an era, the newly developed sports spectacle was taking over.

The sport of hockey had thrown off its small-town Canadian shackles and had – almost overnight – become a massive player on the professional sports market. From a single six-team professional league centred in Eastern Canada and the American Northeast, the sport had ballooned into an increasingly global multi-professional-league monstrosity that took over TV airwaves with its oversized personalities and its unwavering commitment to violence. This was also the era when professional wrestling entered the mainstream discussion, in large part due to the move

from regionally focused mom-and-pop organizations to nation-
ally focused "federations" like the National Wrestling Alliance and
the World Wrestling Federation (now the WWE). In short, it was
an era when the mainstream American sports viewer was widely
accepting of both non-traditional sports and non-traditional
sports entertainment. Both of these tastes, it seemed, linked by
an association with passionate violence, scripted or otherwise.

To add to the Seltzers' problems, during the changeover between Leo and Jerry, another promoter, Bill Griffiths, started
Roller Games in LA, centred around his marquee team, the L.A.
T-Birds (Barbee and Cohen, 24). Although it roughly borrowed
the roller derby rule book, Roller Games took the theatrics to
new heights, emphasizing violence and spectacle over sport.
Through the late '60s both leagues rolled toward the new decade
with varying levels of success and popularity, but their very existence seemed to confuse the crowds who often couldn't, or didn't
bother to, distinguish between the two brands (Storms, 79).

To combat this, Jerry did attempt to spread his teams across
the United States, shaking up rosters and setting up home teams
in major centres outside of San Francisco like Chicago, Cincin-
nati and New York, but by the time the '60s had turned over
into the '70s, roller derby – while still sometimes drawing large
crowds – was hobbling as a business.

Roller derby was also a victim of its own success, and strains
of growing became too much. Although still under singular ownership, by 1970, the teams were spread out across their respective
regions making travel and the running of multiple centres costly,
leading to problems with salary payments. While roller derby had
always been a place of relative equality among men and women
(Deford, 44), during this time some controversy arose over pay-

ment of skaters. Although the Seltzers have always claimed that they paid men and women equally, that is not the story told by some of the skaters (Storms, 79). Mostly though, the anger arose over the payment hierarchy, with skaters like Joanie Weston and Charlie O'Connell making significantly more than newer skaters (Deford, 44); this was enough of an issue that some skaters actually organized a strike in 1972 (Coppage, 88).

Roller derby suffered its first death in 1973, when Jerry Seltzer, wracked with debt, was forced to sell off his teams, beginning with the famous Bay Bombers out of San Francisco (Coppage, 87). There are various reasons given for the demise of roller derby from ticket sales and poor management (Mabe, 48) along with the gas crisis of the early '70s (Barbee and Cohen, 24; Coppage, 91), to problems with an early advanced ticket sales company, Ticketron (Coppage, 94), and even Jerry's divorce (Mabe, 48; Phillips, 230). Jerry gave up the sport slowly, attempting to hold on to as much as he could, but when TV syndication faded, so too did the Seltzer family's carefully crafted monopoly of the sport. On December 8, 1973, the final regular season game of Seltzer-era roller derby was played, ending a thirty-eight-year run (Coppage, 95).

Bill Griffiths, the Seltzers' primary competition in professional roller sports, attempted to keep Roller Games alive beyond roller derby's end by adding more and more spectacle, creating a carnival atmosphere that removed the final elements of the sport from the game and pushed some of derby's great stars, namely Weston and O'Connell, out of the game (Phillips, 230).

By the mid '70s, the first great wave of roller derby had come to a definitive end.

The Attempted Revivals: 1976 – 2000

From about 1976 to the turn of the millennium, various brief attempts were made to return the game to national prominence without much luck. Most notably, Charlie O'Connell, one of the major stars of the Seltzer circuit, tried to bring back a competitive version of the sport in California in the late '70s with limited success (Phillips, 230).

The biggest splash would be made by Bill Griffiths, who had shown that he was not afraid to cross lines to get butts in the seats and eyes on the track. His carnivalized version of the sport, rebranded as *Rock-n-Rollergames*, was broadcast in 1989 and took the theatrics to a level higher (Barbee and Cohen, 25). Using a figure-eight-shaped track with walls, jumps and even a pool of alligators (Mabe, 48), the only sport to the game was in the skaters' ability, as the action was simply professional wrestling on a banked track. With nothing but spectacle to latch onto, the show lasted one season (Mabe, 48).

What followed was the longest span without roller derby in American history, stretching over a decade. But on the cusp of a new millennium, the biggest name in the game returned.

In 1998 Jerry Seltzer re-emerged as commissioner of the World Skating League and backed, once again, by a supportive television network (this time TNN), was set to bring roller derby back to American audiences (Mabe, 51), this time branded as the show *RollerJam*. Along with bringing back Jerry, *RollerJam* also brought in former Seltzer skaters to help train the new generation (Coppage, 108). While this version did initially attempt to bring back the traditional sport in terms of the track and the rules, there was one major difference: it was played on in-line skates. After extensive tryouts that resulted in a group of young, muscled and attractive athletes, the sport was reborn as a six-team league all based out of a massive sound stage at Universal Studies in Orlando, Florida (Barbee and Cohen, 27; Mabe, 54; Coppage, 106).

The show debuted in January 1999, roping in an impressive 2.9 million viewers. This version of the sport did highlight some wonderful athleticism – the skating was outstanding – but even at its very beginnings it skirted the fine line between sport and spectacle. As the ratings began to slip, the theatrics began to ramp up once again. Increasingly, the athleticism was pushed aside for pro-wrestling-style fights and soap-opera-inspired drama, and the women's costumes became skimpier. None of it worked.

Exactly two years after its premiere, in January 2001, *Roller-Jam* was officially cancelled (Barbee and Cohen, 31; Mabe, 58). Although the sport had managed to bridge centuries and limped past the turn of the millennium, with the demise of *RollerJam*, it was once again left for dead.

Despite Jerry's involvement in *RollerJam*, he was never comfortable with any of the revivals. "It was almost tragic what they were doing on the track," he told me when talking about those attempts to rebrand the sport. "It wasn't even *sports*. It was just entertainment." Even though the attempted revivals laid out this pandering to the audience more overtly than the Seltzers ever had, Jerry's criticism may get to the heart of what roller derby was in the twentieth century: even at its most competitive, the integrity of the sport always came second to the need to entertain.

Although Jerry's intentions were always good and his and his father's versions of the game were much closer to sports than any of the others, every incarnation of roller derby to that point had always valued the spectacle over the sport. Even in the late

'60s and early '70s, during the most competitive era of the Seltzer game, when there was actually a regular season and playoff
schedule, fans had little interest in the stats or standings. This
lack of statistical interest was only made worse by television syndication, which had the games airing inconsistently and out of
order (Deford, 26–27). Ironically, it was the money made from
syndication that kept roller derby going as a viable business. But,
to put it simply, the "fans" of the game had never quite become
sports fans, or as sports writer Frank Deford put it at the time,
"They [the fans] are involved in it, not students of it" (7).

From Leo to Jerry to Bill Griffiths, every version of the game
had been built from the top down: from owners down to the skaters. It had always been a carefully crafted entertainment that,
while thriving on the surface, never had much of anything below
that glittery covering. Unlike the other thriving sports of the
century, roller derby had no grassroots. There was no regional
system of local leagues teaching the sport to younger generations
of fans and athletes, there were no farm teams developing better
and better skaters who would eventually replace those at the top,
although the Seltzers did operate training centres. Despite having all the trappings of traditional sports broadcasts, even the
televised versions of the game acted as an advertisement to draw
people to the live events, making those experiences a once-a-year
spectacle. Roller derby undeniably had its moments of popularity, but in every single example it was top heavy in organization
and execution, and its weak infrastructure destined the sport to
topple over.

the great leap backwards

2009 AND THE DEFINING OF FLAT TRACK ROLLER DERBY

In March 2010 Toronto Roller Derby's travel team, CN Power, hosted what was essentially an unofficial Canadian championship. The two-day tournament, called the Quad City Chaos, featured the four top teams in Canada at the time. Hammer City's Eh! Team, Montreal's New Skids on the Block and Vancouver's Terminal City All-Stars joined Toronto for a round robin tournament.

After a more than two-year apprenticeship as a superfan of the game, I had finally dived in. My blog had been launched and, along with Dawson, I had helped to form ToRD.TV, which we'd hoped would turn into a video-based site featuring streamed games, interviews and other features. I'd written an extensive preview of the tournament and was set to film highlights and conduct interviews with skaters throughout the weekend. I had big expectations for the tournament and for Montreal's performance in particular, so I knew that this was going to be an important and potentially surprising weekend. I was also beginning to get a sense that fans in Canada were not ready for what was to occur. From debate among the local community and comments on my blog, I knew that everyone was expecting a close, competitive tournament. They were clearly not ready for the heightened level of play that Montreal was about to bring to the track.

One of the most anticipated moments of that first Quad City Chaos was the opening game between Hammer City and Montreal. Within the past year, both had become the first Canadian, and first international, members of the Women's Flat Track Derby Association, which meant that they were going to be a part of the WFTDA's ranking system and were eligible to compete for a spot in the association's annual playoffs. This was undoubtedly a historic game: the first WFTDA-sanctioned game in Canada, and the first between two non-US teams.

Montreal had been on somewhat of a tear at the end of 2009 and the beginning of 2010, playing anyone and everyone and going wherever they needed to go to do so. In the weeks leading up to the Quad City Chaos they'd gone on a two-game weekend road trip to Arizona, followed by a three-game road trip down the east coast of the US. There weren't many ways to watch roller derby online back then, but I'd followed the live blogs (called textcasts) on the Derby News Network and live twitter updates of Montreal's games and knew that they were soaking up new slow-style strategies that were just being developed south of the border and had yet to reach Canada. By the time they rolled into Toronto in March, they had become a changed team.

The Hamilton-Montreal showdown was a very early Saturday morning game at ToRD's Hangar; there were only insiders and superfans lining the track for this highly anticipated moment. The first hint that something might be different came while watching Montreal warm up. They began their warm-up off skates, which was unprecedented at the time, and even in warm-up fatigues it was easy to see that they were fitter and stronger than everyone else. Roller derby, certainly in Canada, was still deeply cloaked in its punk rock attitude and the notion of working out off skates to improve on-skates performance was new. It seemed to many skaters to be a waste of valuable track time. But there was Montreal, running laps around the space, doing leaps and stretches and planks.

Within a few minutes of the opening whistle of that first game, it was clear that this was not going to be a pretty sight. Montreal dominated from the start; they baffled Hammer City with strange play, alternating blazing speed with grinding slowness, an intentional duality that had never been witnessed in the Canadian game before. During the first New Skids power jam, when the Hammer City jammer was in the penalty box, the relentless Montreal blockers isolated a lone Hammer City blocker and then held her behind her counterparts who struggled to stay in play (i.e., to remain part of the pack). The jammer sped by the stopped skaters and Hammer City could only watch it all unfold, bewildered. Whatever game Montreal was playing was not the same as the one being played by their opponents. For almost all in attendance it was unnerving and confusing, for some, even infuriating. It was one of the most exciting moments of my sports-fan life.

Within the previous eighteen months, Montreal's and Hamilton's travel teams had met twice in thrilling, incredibly closely matched contests. Montreal had been able to pull off both wins – but just barely – with fairly regular scores for the time: 58–48 and then 84–80. A combined difference of fourteen points over two games.

When the final whistle blew in that WFTDA-sanctioned game at the Quad City Chaos in March 2010 in Toronto, the scoreboard read 208–26.

Montreal would go on to beat Vancouver and Toronto with similar ease that weekend. Never before had one Canadian team so thoroughly dominated another, and especially not teams that shared such a similar history. But the game had changed: it had changed quickly and it had changed remarkably and it was obvious that many teams had some catching up to do.

After seven years of existence, flat track roller derby had finally been born.

★ ★ ★

It was harder to see at the time, but in retrospect it's pretty clear that in the world of flat track roller derby everything changed in 2009.

I first became aware of the monumental changes on Saturday, November 21, 2009, at my uncle and aunt's house in Ajax, Ontario – a suburb east of Toronto. I was sitting in front of a computer in their dining room, my family assembled to celebrate the birthdays of both my sister and me. The WFTDA Championships were being boutcast on the Derby News Network live from Philadelphia and I really wanted to catch a few quarterfinal matches, in particular I wanted to watch the Denver Roller Dolls and the Oly Rollers play in their respective games.

Although I was already a big fan of the local game, roller derby for me was not exactly a spectator sport yet. I wasn't fully aware of the extent of the community outside of Canada's borders; I was just starting to get straight the names of the early stars of the game. But also, at that stage in the growth of the sport, there wasn't really that much difference between the teams playing at the highest level and at the level that I'd been watching. They may have been fitter and slightly better skaters, but they were all playing the same straightforward game: skate fast, turn left, hit your opponents and try to avoid the same. Of course, up until that point, there also hadn't been much of an opportunity to watch those top-level teams without actually going to whatever city or town they were playing in. But with the advent of roller derby live streaming in 2009, these increasingly legendary teams were now accessible to anyone with access to the Internet.

This wasn't the first year that the WFTDA playoffs were boutcast by Hurt Reynolds, Gnosis and the crew at DNN, but compared to 2008 – the first year they'd duct taped and fumbled their way to a live stream – there was so much more viewership and focus on the game. Drew Barrymore's *Whip It* had come out, launching the careers of many Babe Ruthlesses[2] in small towns all across the US and Canada, and creating an audience for the sport's most competitive teams.

At the fourth WFTDA playoffs in 2009, for the first time there was a visual separation of the way those top teams played the game compared to the rest. At the time, the WFTDA was organized into four regions – North Central, South Central, East and West – with the top twelve from each region invited to participate in single-elimination regional playoff tournaments every fall. The top three teams from each regional playoff tournament then went on to play for the Hydra, the trophy given to the winner of the twelve-team WFTDA Championship tournament.

One of the storylines that was dominating the tournament going into that 2009 championship weekend was the story of the Oly Rollers. Playing out of Olympia, Washington, they were a team that consisted of towering roller derby machines that emerged, or so it seemed, from out of nowhere to rewrite the early WFTDA record books. For us in Canada, that season was the first time derby gossip grew to a point where it was heard outside of the narrow confines of the tournaments themselves, and Oly had already built a reputation. The gossip said that they weren't friendly with the other teams, they didn't compete with everyone to win the after-party; they were business-like, focused. They came in, did their business (winning) and left.

As facts about who they actually were and where they'd come from began to emerge, I could see that they simply weren't "derby girls," as most skaters identified at the time. They were, to be blunt, jocks, with fairly extensive sports backgrounds. The core of the Oly Rollers was built of a group of women who'd risen through the ranks of USA Roller Sports (USARS) in a variety of disciplines, but primarily hockey (Sassy, Tannibal Lector, Hockey Honey) and speed skating (Atomatrix), not to mention a trio of sisters, led by jammer Blonde 'N Bitchin', who'd literally grown up in their family's roller rink in Washington State. In other words, they'd been raised in a sports culture where tournaments were places you went to compete and hopefully win, defined by long drives, generic hotel rooms and unfamiliar venues that in their universality leant a certain familiarity to them. They were athletes first, or so it seemed, and derby girls second. They didn't even wear their derby names on their uniforms, which was baffling to me at the time, considering the pride with which the skaters I knew carried their monikers.

The roller derby revival had less athletic roots than the Oly Rollers, but by Gotham's 2008 championship victory, it had begun to reveal an athletic avant-garde who were pushing for a more competitive game. The Oly Rollers defined this transition in 2009. They were incredibly fast, fit and focused. A lifetime on skates, both in-line and quads, had made them phenomenal skaters. That year they entered the tournament as the top seed from the west and were on an 8–0 run in the WFTDA, 14–0 overall dating back to the previous year, their first as a roller derby team. They played a simple but effective style of hit-and-run roller derby: they skated fast, made holes for their jammer when she needed it and knocked the hell out of the opposition jammer. They had more strength, speed and endurance than anyone else, so despite the team's strategic simplicity, they were quite effective.

But the Oly Rollers were not the only story to emerge from that year's playoff run. Another story had begun to take shape on the Friday night of the tournament and had started to seep out over social networks, threatening to overtake the Oly story as the dominant narrative of the weekend. People had been talking about Denver, who'd slipped into the tournament as the third ranked team from the west, and their unpopular strategic tactics. Most shocking for me – someone still very much in the throes of initial love for the overly inclusive good-naturedness of the sport – was that the fans in Philly's Pennsylvania Convention Center had apparently booed Denver in their one-sided upset over the popular 2007 champs, Kansas City, the night before.

The Denver Roller Dolls had not made much of an impression on the larger roller derby community yet; they weren't even the best team in their city. They entered the tournament as the second team from the Mile High City, part of a league that had formed in opposition to Denver's original league, the Rocky Mountain Rollergirls. The first shocking aspect about the Denver story had nothing to do with on-track action: they had their real names on their slick, sporty jerseys. This seemed stranger to me even than Oly's decision to not have names on their uniforms – at least the Oly Rollers had derby names, even if they didn't flaunt them. Denver had dropped the derby name completely and the names on their backs read as the seemingly banal Adams, Akers, James, Preston and Rivas.

Friday night at the 2009 Champs featured a play-in game between the regions' second- and third-ranked teams, vying for an opportunity to meet up with one of the four top seeds in the sudden-death quarterfinals the next morning. Coming into the tournament, Denver wasn't seen as a threat and wasn't even expected to progress past that opening round game against the heavily favoured KC team who'd topped them in their previous meeting, but from the opening whistle, Denver began to use tactics that frustrated Kansas City and baffled the fans. At the time, a single whistle blast released the pack and when those skaters crossed the pivot line, a second whistle released the jammers. Only Denver refused to pass over the pivot line until Kansas City did, meaning that they would have the defensive position at the back of the pack. As the jam clock ticked away with the teams barely moving and jockeying for position at the pivot line, the crowd became restless, nearly a quarter of the jam-time had elapsed before the jammers were released. In the first half, Denver played the back of the pack with a deliberate purpose and plan that no one had ever seen in the game before. They controlled their defence so specifically that their jammer often pushed the other team's pack ahead and "out of play" (farther than twenty feet [six metres] from the pack), thereby destroying the pack and incurring pack destruction penalties, as skaters have to maintain the pack at all times. On second (scoring) passes when they had lead, Denver blockers began to try to trap a Kansas City blocker behind them to keep the pack moving as slowly as possible.

All of this was relayed through often angry Facebook posts and an exploding comments section on DNN. A Denver jammer, Heather Juska, had picked up a rarely heard of twenty-five points on a power jam. Although within two years, thirty- and even forty-point jams would become common, at the time it was a shocking number, especially for that level of play. It was intriguing. This team skating under real names and employing specific slow, "trick," strategies to upset teams. I couldn't picture it.

So at my own birthday party, I was rude and stepped away from my family, sat in front of a computer and turned on Derby News Network to catch the 2009 WFTDA Championship quarterfinals between Denver and Chicago's Windy City Rollers.

The defining moment came late in the first half of that game against Windy City: Denver had a small lead, but the game had been back and forth to that point. Eventually, a Windy City jammer penalty provided an opportunity for Denver to extend its lead, as with a jammer in the penalty box, only the opposing team is able to score. Once again, the Denver blockers tried to isolate a single Chicago blocker. When they managed to do so, they slowed the pack almost to a standstill and – with the other Windy City blockers too far ahead of the pack to do anything legally, as they'd skated away from the stopped pack, putting themselves all out of play – the Denver jammer easily lapped them for five points.

Predictably, the trapped blocker skated backwards in an attempt to escape the Denver swarm, but unpredictably – at least to everyone in attendance and watching on computers across North America and some specific parts of the globe – the Denver pack quickly leaped backwards to follow her, chase her even, in the opposite direction of gameplay. To stay in play, to remain within twenty feet (six metres) of the pack, the blockers at the front had to turn around and rush backwards toward them. All the while the Denver jammer was skating laps untouched.

Denver pulled ahead significantly on a few huge power jams. They would hold off Windy City for the major upset over the top ranked team from the North Central Region. Given the stage, it was the biggest upset the sport had ever seen.

Denver hadn't been the first team to employ what came to be derisively known as slow derby strategy, or, to some, simply Denver Strategy. It's been traced back to Albuquerque's Duke City Derby, who, as ironic legend has it, developed the strategy in an attempt to counter faster teams, specifically, according to former Duke City skater Muffin, to counter their rival Denver's superior speed. Denver, a team blessed with speed, didn't complain about the unconventional strategy being used against them, instead, they perfected it and added it to their broadening playbook.

I was astonished, watched rapt as it all unfolded in front of me. It would take some time to come together coherently, but I knew that the game of flat track roller derby had been laid out clearly for all of us to see. For the first time ever, flat track roller derby had truly separated itself from the banked track versions that had preceded it. Teams now realized that the strategies that had defined the game for generations would not be suitable for this version of the sport. It was the beginning of the evolution of the flat track game, when strategies would arise organically from the surface and the elements that went with it – such as boundaries both inside and out, and the ease with which one could change pace and move laterally. It also began a massive evolution in the rules of flat track roller derby, further pushing this new version of the game away from its banked track antecedents.

Since the first official flat track game in April 2003 to those playoffs in 2009, flat track roller derby had been *flat track roller derby* in name only, and only because it was played on a flat surface. The sport itself had basically been a banked track version of the game being played without a bank: Skate forward, skate fast, turn left. It was a game plan perfectly suited to a velodrome, but that seemed antithetical to playing the game on a flat surface. Because the sport of roller derby had originally evolved on a banked surface, speed had always been perceived as an intrinsic part of the game. But this is a limiting and even false assumption when applied to a flat track. At the time, this was a somewhat controversial stance, but one that people, particularly the international derby community, have come to embrace.

Think about the objective of the game: The purpose of roller derby is to score more points than the opposing team. Points are achieved by one team advancing its jammer past the opposing team's blockers. Logically then, the best way to advance the jammer past the opposing blockers in as efficient a way as possible is to slow those blockers down. On the flip side, the best way to avoid being scored on is to speed up and keep your hips, and therefore your *point*, ahead of the opposing jammer. It seems obvious to me that as much as flat track roller derby is a fast game, it is also a slow one. With all else being equal, the team best able to balance these elements, to control the pace of the game, is the team that will succeed. This has been a truth in flat track roller derby since those 2009 playoffs.

In November of 2009, a great conflation of DNN's live streaming, the Oly Rollers' athleticism and Denver's strategic evolution all came together to alter the evolutionary course of the flat track game. A simple stepping backwards and forcing an out-of-bounds skater to race clockwise in anti-derby direction to legally re-enter the track behind the skater who forced her out changed the sport forever. Things were messy for the next few years as teams figured this out: those teams that adapted quickly, as Montreal had, became the dominant teams in the game, those who were slow to embrace the new strategies fell to the wayside or suffered brutal, unprecedented blowouts like the ones we'd seen at the Quad City Chaos in March 2010.

Denver would shake up the derby community by coming out of nowhere to capture a stunning third-place finish at the 2009 WFTDA Championship tournament, while the Oly Rollers would roll their way to the 2009 title and continue their record-setting winning streak for nearly another full season.

Although the changes to the game would not be without controversy or resistance and would take years to iron out – really, ironing out this fast-slow duality has become the central focus and aspect of the development of the flat track game – after the winter of '09, the sport of flat track roller derby had changed irrevocably.

The irony is apparent: Flat track roller derby had experienced its great leap forward all because some skaters saw the logic in taking a great leap backwards.

nerding out

THE FIVE KEY MOMENTS IN THE DEVELOPMENT OF COMPETITIVE CANADIAN ROLLER DERBY

During the years between 2006 and 2011, the sport of flat track roller derby experienced a period of unbelievable growth. Specifically, it experienced incredible growth in the number of people playing and the amount of nations it was played in. But beyond that logistical growth, there was also incredible growth in the competitive level that the sport was being played at.

The year 2006 represents a real turning point for the game; by the end of the year the game would grow beyond the US and would pop up in Canada, England, Germany, Australia and New Zealand. It would also be the first year of the WFTDA and its annual championship tournament. The next half-decade would plant the seeds for the future of the game.

Mirroring these changes were the changes that were occurring in Canada. The transition from birth to adolescence (and maybe adulthood!) all happened in Canada during that five-year stretch. Specifically, over this five-year period there were five key events that had a massive impact on the game in Canada.

1. Betties' D-Day
August 19, 2006, George Bell Arena, Toronto, ON

Take three of Canada's earliest leagues, throw them together in an iceless arena on a hot summer day in August 2006, and what you get is the event out of which all other Canadian roller derby events are born. Yes, there were stirrings of leagues in Edmonton, Vancouver and even Vancouver Island at that point, but they lacked the one advantage that the leagues in Toronto, Hamilton and Montreal had: proximity.

This event, set up as a tournament, would mark the first games for a majority of the skaters in each of the three leagues. Even calling them leagues is being generous. At that point, only Hammer City had actually held a public event and had two teams in its league. Montreal had not even named teams yet and for this event divided its skaters into two squads, called the Cougars and the Felines. Toronto Roller Derby didn't exist, but the two teams in Toronto took part: the hosting Smoke City Betties and the Toronto Terrors. However, the Terrors had split its ever-increasing membership into four teams.

The first game at the tournament featured the Hamilton Harlots and one of the Terrors' offspring, the Death Track Dolls, with the Hammer City skaters giving a lesson in derby to their slightly less experienced counterparts, winning the short twenty-minute game 34–11. The Harlots' league mates, the Steel Town Tank Girls, proved equally dominant, crushing another Terrors' offshoot, the Deadly Viper Assassination Squad (D-VAS), in the first round. The Harlots got some revenge after their recent loss to the Tank Girls when they took them down in the semifinal, before going on to defeat one of the surprising Montreal split-squad teams, the Cougars, in the final. The host, Smoke City

Betties, set up the day so that the winner of the tournament would take them on in a full-length marquee game. Although the Betties gave the Harlots all that they could handle in that matchup, the Hammer City skaters continued their winning streak by taking out the hosts, 79–57.

For practical purposes, the importance of this event was obvious. The three leagues learned how to put on games, saw what those games would look like, figured out the needs in terms of both on-skate (referees) and non-skating officials (NSOs), and all the other practicalities that needed to be accounted for at this early stage of development – the game was still so new and the understanding so raw, that many in attendance had never actually seen a game.

But this tournament would also provide the stirrings of what is commonly referred to as the community; it would provide those links between the skaters that they would need to plan future games and tournaments, it would build bonds and friendships that would foster the growth of early Canadian roller derby. Similarly, it provided the first example of the tournament model that would prove so important for the growth of the sport, not only in Ontario, but everywhere in the country that roller derby would be played.

2. Derby Night in Canada
August 23, 2008, Minoru Arena, Richmond, BC

Nearly two years to the day after Canada's first house league tournament was played, Vancouver's Terminal City All-Stars hosted the first-ever travel team tournament, aptly titled Derby Night in Canada.

As much as D-Day ushered flat track derby into Canada, Derby Night in Canada kicked off the competitive era of the

EIGHT-WHEELED FREEDOM

sport in the country. Travel team derby, although happening
since roughly 2004 south of the border, had just taken hold in
Canada. The tournament featured Terminal City, Montreal's
New Skids on the Block, the Calgary Roller Derby Association
All Stars and two teams from Victoria, the Eves of Destruction
and Victoria Rollergirls.

With a victory over Edmonton nearly a year previous and
victories in this tournament over the two Victoria teams and
Calgary, Terminal City had proven itself the top team in the
West; similarly, Montreal that summer had knocked off travel
teams from Toronto and Hamilton to prove itself the mighti-
est in the East. Although not a full-length bout, Terminal City
would defeat Montreal 66–48 in the tournament final to lay
claim to being the top team in Canada.[3] While the Eves remain
a strong league in Victoria, they would never reach the travel-
team heights of their mainland counterparts, and it would take
Calgary another six years before they really became a player in
the competitive circuit.

But more important than the results, this tournament brought
Canada into the travel-team era, a starting point that would
present a model for leagues to build on. Eventually, it would lead
teams to WFTDA membership, then to increased travel south
of the border and then to the WFTDA playoffs, the highest level
of competition that the sport has to offer.

As an event, it would also have a direct influence on the next
key moment in the development of competitive roller derby in
this country.

3. Quad City Chaos 2010

March 27-28, 2010, The Hangar at Downsview Park, Toronto, ON

If Derby Night ushered in the travel-team era, than the inaugural QCC took the competition to a whole new level. A four-team round-robin tournament featuring Hammer City's Eh! Team, Montreal's New Skids on the Block, Terminal City's All-Stars and Toronto's CN Power, this tournament was important for a number of reasons: it featured the four best teams in the country at the time; it included the first WFTDA-sanctioned game held outside of the US and the first featuring two international combatants; and, finally, it introduced flat track pace strategies to Canadian roller derby. Quite literally, the sport would never be the same in this country after this event.

On the track, the host Toronto team notched a win over Hammer City, but it was a narrow one, 89–87, and they would also narrowly defeat Vancouver's Terminal City, who ended up winless on the weekend. But the three incredibly competitive games featuring Terminal City, Toronto and Hammer City were overshadowed by Montreal's absolute and complete dominance. Just to put into perspective how far ahead Montreal was from everyone else at the time: the average point differential in the games between Hamilton, Toronto and Vancouver was a paltry ten points; meanwhile, Montreal won its three games by an average of one hundred fifty-seven points per game.

That supplies another key reason why this tournament was so important for competitive derby in Canada: Montreal brought the future of the flat track game to the country that weekend, providing a few of the best teams in the nation a glimpse of what the future would entail. It was strange to watch the games at the time, watching Montreal physically and strategically dominate everyone. It presented a clear divide between teams and even skaters: you could play the game for fun, or you could play the game to compete. Those two notions had been interchangeable in Canada up to that point.

After March 2010, strapping on skates and wearing the same uniform was not enough to remain a competitive team anymore. Now, at the highest level, the sport was going to require athleticism and strategy. Since that weekend Vancouver and Toronto have followed Montreal's lead and become competitors in the WFTDA's top division, while Hammer City didn't quite have the organizational drive, or the population pool to pull from, to remain on par. The pace strategies so awkwardly and painfully introduced that weekend eventually became commonplace in the sport and in Canada, and the Quad City Chaos has remained an important annual event, eventually becoming the first full WFTDA tournament in the country and then the first full WFTDA Division 1 event as well.

4. The 2010 WFTDA Eastern Region Playoffs
September 24 – 26, 2010, Westchester County Center, White Plains, NY

On September 24, 2010, Montreal's New Skids on the Block made flat track roller derby history when they laced up against their increasingly intense rivals Boston for a quarterfinal showdown in the WFTDA's Eastern Region playoffs. It was the fifth year of the WFTDA playoffs, and Montreal, qualifying sixth out of the twelve teams in the Eastern Region tournament, had become the first non-US-based team to play in them.

Montreal Roller Derby distanced itself from its Canadian peers in 2010, but then again, the team distanced itself from a lot of teams in 2010. The Neon Army, so named because of their loud multi-coloured neon uniforms, had skated to an 11–3 record that season, notching big wins against Tampa, DC and Arizona. More importantly in the Great White North, the roller derby community now had a reason to pay attention to the WFTDA and its regular season and playoff systems. The timing couldn't have been better.

This was the second year that the Derby News Network would broadcast the entire playoffs and there was a slowly growing global interest in the games. For pretty much the first time, the derby community was seeing the game being played at a level that was no longer comparable to their local version. The teams in the playoffs, and particularly those top twelve teams that would qualify for the championship tournament, were playing at a completely different level strategically and athletically from everyone else. And because Montreal was involved, there were plenty of Canadian eyes trained on the playoffs for the first time.

Montreal would lose that quarterfinal game to the higher ranked Boston and be relegated to the Consolation Bracket that they were expected to dominate, and for the most part, they did, crushing the Dutchland Derby Rollers from Lancaster, Pennsylvania, by two hundred sixty-five points before Raleigh's Carolina Rollergirls scored a controversial last-gasp two-point win over Montreal that would begin a string of heartbreaking playoff losses that would plague this generation of Montreal skaters. I'll never forget those final moments of the Carolina game and the somewhat controversial jammer-penalty call that would end Montreal's chances. It was the first time I ever yelled at a television screen over a roller derby game, but certainly not the last.

Montreal's appearance would resonate even beyond the borders of Canada. In 2011, London, England, would qualify for the playoffs and they would meet up with Montreal in the first all-international WFTDA playoff game in the consolation final of the 2011 Eastern Region tournament.[4]

While the number of international teams has continued to increase every subsequent year after that and has become commonplace, it all started with Montreal in White Plains, New York, in 2010.

5. The 2011 *Blood & Thunder* Roller Derby World Cup
December 4–6, 2011, The Bunker at Downsview Park, Toronto, ON

By the end of the 2011 season, everyone in the international roller derby community knew that Canucks could play, but in December of that year, they would also learn that stereotypically mild-mannered Canadians could also throw a party.

Toronto had been hand-picked by roller derby magazine *Blood & Thunder* to host the first-ever Roller Derby World Cup and during the first week of December 2011, thirteen roller derby teams representing their respective nations touched down in Toronto to play in the sport's first world championship.

Globally, flat track roller derby had gone through its second wave of growth in 2010 and '11, a trend that was evident on more local levels as well. Still riding the cresting wave of the *Whip It* bump, the sport in Canada had grown exponentially and its national team represented that. Although criticized at the time for favouring regional representation over putting together the best possible team, the national team selection process, a series of three regional tryouts, had worked to spread awareness about all of the leagues sprouting up across our vast country and there was skater representation from coast to coast on the squad.

The team – led by a core of Montreal skaters – as expected, did very well, eventually losing to USA, also as expected, in the final by a monstrous score of 336–33. Despite the lopsided score, it was a proud moment for Canadian roller derby, as, believe it or not, the three hundred thirty-six points the Americans had scored was the fewest they'd managed to gain in the whole tournament, and Canada's thirty-three points were more than had been scored against the US in all of its previous games *combined*.

More important for Canadian roller derby, the event, which was of course broadcast on DNN, unified and focused a national roller derby community. Competitively, it gave skaters across the country a goal to strive for that went well beyond simply making their home league's travel team. Eventually, the national program would inspire the formation of provincial teams as a means of providing a stepping stone to the higher echelons of international competitive derby. The first would sprout up in Alberta and Saskatchewan, quickly followed by Ontario, Manitoba and New Brunswick.

And of course, the first-ever World Cup would provide a lasting Canadian-centric global landmark for the sport.

smack daddy and the new skids

ROLLER DERBY AS *THE* SPORT OF THIRD-WAVE FEMINISM

Like many others across Canada in 2008, I'd found roller derby in one of a growing number of arenas across the country where the sport was played live. By the time I stumbled into Arena Saint-Louis in Montreal, you could watch the beginnings of leagues in cities like Victoria, Calgary, Ottawa, London and Kitchener-Waterloo on top of the larger leagues already established in Vancouver, Edmonton, Toronto and Hamilton.

But before those early leagues existed, there was no way to watch roller derby live. For many of that first wave of Canadian roller derby skaters, the first glimpse they had of the roller derby revival came when, on January 2, 2006, A&E broadcast the North American debut of *Rollergirls*.

Produced by Gary and Julie Auerbach, the show aired in winter and spring of 2006, chronicling a single season in the lives of the TXRD Lonestar Rollergirls, an old-school-style banked track roller derby league in Austin, Texas. Told initially, and primarily, through the point of view of a skater playing in her first season with a team called the Putas Del Fuego, it focused more on the lifestyles of the skaters than the skating itself. It was big on the inter-skater drama, but low on skating specifics, big on the spectacle of the banked track events, and low on analyzing on-track strategies and gameplay. As a reality-TV-style look at the lives of the colourful skaters, *Rollergirls* was a compelling show: dramatic and easily digestible. But it was far from being a show about a sport, and it's actually quite possible to watch the full series and come away with very little knowledge of the game beyond which position scores the points. And yet, many Canadian skaters cite it as the inspiration for their interest in the game.

The opening sequences of the show pretty much reaffirm any stereotype you may have of roller derby as a sports spectacle, with skaters in skimpy outfits parading around the track to punk music and spanking each other or shooting at the crowd with toy guns. There are cheerleaders decked out in all black with matte-black pompoms. There are wacky announcers.

But the viewer's entryway into the story is through a very normal looking, seemingly shy, dark-haired girl who watches from the margins. When the skaters enter the track, something noticeable changes on her face as she registers the gameplay. It seems to capture the idea of the moment of a calling, but then in voice-over she reveals that she is actually a nervous rookie, Venus Envy, scouting her more experienced competition. She is still wrapped in those early moments of infatuation with the game and has put everything else in her life on hold to pursue the sport and the ever-expanding culture around it.

It doesn't take long into the show to realize that everything in the Thunderdome, a warehouse that has been converted into a roller derby stadium, has been built by the skaters and is run by the skaters. One hundred per cent of the spectacle, from the track to the uniforms to the names to the rules being followed, is of their making.

The show itself didn't do that well and was cancelled after a single season, but it became the kind of show that in the mid-2000s was endlessly burned on DVDs and passed around. The copy I have was given to me by Montreal Roller Derby's Low Dive Jenny and may have actually been burned for her by someone else before it got into my hands. But for a show that barely made a stir in the crowded North American market, it had quite a profound influence around the continent. There was something about the women in the show, who were fiercely independent, powerful and fearless that made them attractive to women viewers. It could be argued that North America in 2006 was primed for something like this.

I've often asked myself what it was that led me and my partner to alter the course of our lives for a game. In those early days, it wasn't necessarily the sport. It was largely baffling to me, and at the time very unsophisticated strategically, but with complex rules and levels of penalties that were impenetrable. It was probably a confluence of things.

In the summer of 2006, Dawson and I had just moved to Montreal, returning from a three-year stint living and travelling abroad, much of it spent in Asia. The dawn of a new century is a strange time to be away and upon return it felt as if something had changed. It seemed as though we'd missed the birth of the twenty-first century. Roller derby seemed like something specifically from this new era.

Although Dawson and I have different relationships with sports and sports culture, we do have similar backgrounds in one way: we were both raised by single mothers and surrounded in our youths by dominant female presences. In many ways – however heightened and more playful – the qualities that had attracted us to roller derby were the qualities that could define our own mothers. What we saw on the track were women who shared the principles of our upbringings: They were principled, stubborn, fiercely independent, and confident. In Arena Saint-Louis we'd found a space and a sport that not only fostered these qualities but that celebrated them.

For us then, seeing that matriarchal world view played out so overtly in a distinct and unique subculture was inspiring. Especially in those early days, when the sport was figuring itself out, that subculture would provide the main allure that would fuel the rapid spread of modern roller derby in the early to mid 2000s. And while the expansion of social networking and web streaming provided a massive boost for the growth of the game, it was this women-centric community, and the perceived freedoms that would be celebrated in it, that drew in the early skaters and built the foundations for the sport. Sport was, arguably, the one dominant pop culture arena that third-wave feminism had yet to truly find a foothold in, and at that late stage in the pluralistic feminist third wave, the culture was ready for a sport to define it. As much as it was an extension of other third-wave feminisms, with its roots in punk rock and its unwavering DIY ethic, roller derby may well have been the first third-wave feminist sport.

Feminist theory is one example where social philosophies have far outstripped the reality on the ground. In the late 1990s pop culture and theoretical thinking had already begun to move well into the third wave. Yet, if second-wave feminism is loosely defined as the era in which women fought for institutional and legal equality, it is easy to argue that second-wave feminism in professional or competitive sports didn't see its successes until the 1990s, when women were finally accepted as viable professional athletes.

The '90s saw a massive growth of participation for women at the professional or international level in soccer and two of the Big Four North American sports, generally considered to be football, baseball, basketball and hockey. In 1990, the International Ice Hockey Federation (IIHF) held its first-ever Women's World Championships, spurring massive growth in participation that saw the number of women playing hockey increase by four hundred per cent from 1990 to 2003, leading to the sport's inclusion at the 1998 Olympics (Parker and White, 10). The Fédération International de Football Association (FIFA) followed suit in 1991 with the inaugural Women's World Cup, while the Women's National Basketball Association (WNBA) was formed in 1996, opening its doors to the public the following year. Globally, the 1996 Atlanta Olympics also provided a boon for attention on female athletics. In *Built to Win: The Female Athlete as Cultural Icon*, Leslie Heywood and Shari L. Dworkin note that the 1996 Olympics were the first to focus on female athletes as athletes first (26). They also note that this was reflecting a greater trend in culture as well, as 1995 marked the first time that women bought more athletic footwear than men (31), for example.

However, there was a price paid for providing this foundational framework, and the women of this important era in sport were working within the constraints of male-developed and -dominated sports. Their advancements were great, yes, and it put female athletes on a stage never seen before, but they were doing it by playing feminized versions of so-called men's sports. Women's hockey, for example, is literally a watered-down version of the men's game, played with a modified rule set that allows for only limited physical contact. In a pure reflection of the gender framing of these sports, the Canadian women at the first Ice Hockey Women's World Championship in 1990 were given Team Canada jerseys that were incredibly similar to the men's versions save for one major difference: all of the red had been changed to a soft pink.

Sport has always had a delayed reaction to not only feminist movements but progressive movements as a whole. American social critic and professor Michael Messner calls sport culture the "last institutional bastion of men's traditional power and privilege" (165). Therefore, sport is often the final place where progress can be seen in mainstream culture; once a regressive act becomes taboo in sports culture, it is usually a good sign that significant progress is being made in culture at large. For example, take the Toronto Blue Jays' Yunel Escobar and the uproar that erupted in summer 2013 when he wrote a Spanish homophobic slur on his eye black (he was shipped out of town shortly thereafter), or the National Hockey League's participation in the You Can Play campaign encouraging LGBTQ kids to don skates to play hockey. Both examples reflect shifting Canadian attitudes toward the LGBTQ community.

Heywood and Dworkin also note that there was a significant pushback by conservative culture occurring in the early 2000s toward the rise of women's sports (43–44), and despite the continued, modest success of the WNBA, no professional women's soccer or hockey league has managed to survive with any sort of consistency. Whether the product was good or not did not seem to matter to the growth, or lack thereof, for these sports; they were getting absolutely no coverage from the sports networks or news outlets. From 1989 to 2004, the percentage of women's sports covered on network sports news shows remained virtually unchanged, barely rising from 5–6% over that period despite the extensive growth of women's athletics during that time (Messner, 156).

At the same time, the athletes in these sports who garnered the most media attention were generally those who exhibited the traits most easily digestible to mainstream viewers: they exhibited the hallmarks of heterosexual femininity and attractiveness (Chananie-Hill, Waldron and Umsted, 36; Messner, 165; Wilson, 227). Because of the rigid confines of patriarchy established around these sports and their supporting infrastructures, women who wanted to be involved often had to check their feminism at the door (Heywood and Dworkin, 50).

American sociologist Nancy J. Finley, in her paper "Skating Femininity: Gender Maneuvering in Women's Roller Derby," also writes about how women playing sports in the newly established Big Three, instead of carving a truly feminist path, were unwittingly acting to help maintain or strengthen the establishment of what she calls hegemonic masculinity as the dominant world view or order. These feminized versions of popular male sports reinforced that the men's game is the superior or "real" version of the game (367). In many ways then, the development of these professional sports only acted to prop up the male athlete as the superior player (Finley, 361). To put it crudely, allowing women to play these modified (feminized) versions of sports acted as a way to keep women marginalized. On top of that, women who were more traditionally feminine were given extra privileges, not to mention screen time, than those who were not (Parker and White, 18).

Although she never explicitly states that roller derby is *the* sport of third-wave feminism, Nancy Finley does say that the sport uses the tools of the third wave to disrupt gender conditioning and that the sport offers a progressive "alternative femininity" (373). She also points out that "predictable gender relations in sports are disrupted when the feminine evoked is not complementary to established masculine position in sports" (373). From its beginnings in the early 2000s and certainly when it began to spread rapidly across North America between 2006 and 2008, flat track roller derby's presentation was rooted in a near carnivalesque parody of women and gender relations. This is one thing that is made abundantly clear in the early episodes of *Rollergirls* and becomes reflected in all the early versions of contemporary women's roller derby.

In their 2012 essay "Third-Wave Agenda: Women's Flat-Track Roller Derby," Ruth Chananie-Hill, Jennifer Waldron and Natalie Umsted attempt to define third-wave feminism, while acknowledging the near impossibility of the task, and roller derby's place within it. They do manage to document four key themes of third-wave feminism as a way to separate it from its predecessors:

1. Fluidity and freedom of gender and sexual expression.
2. All-encompassing inclusiveness regardless of gender, sex, appearance, ability, ethnicity, race, sexual preference, etc.
3. Concern with multiple social justice issues and connecting global to local.
4. Individual expression through the sharing of personal narratives. (34)

It's not at all difficult to see these themes playing out in the early stages of the development of contemporary roller derby. The writers conclude that not only does roller derby adhere to the principles of third-wave feminism but is actually helping to "shape the third-wave model of sport" (Chananie-Hill, Waldron and Umsted, 46) and that it "is transforming and will continue to transform sport" (47). While these scholars link roller derby to sports such as women's rugby, lesbian soccer and feminist softball leagues (45), women's flat track roller derby – from its often makeshift settings to the derby names, from the propensity toward fishnets and absurd uniforms early on in the revival to the playing of punk or riot grrrl genre music during gameplay – refuses to bend to the expectations of traditional sports culture and remains distinct in its lack of a masculine, patriarchal antecedent, making it truly the first and perhaps defining sport of third-wave feminism.

I saw this playing out in Montreal when I first stumbled upon the game, with its distinct announcer, its powerful, yet sometimes distinctly or exaggeratedly feminine, participants and, almost indefinably, the attitude. And at the time, the flat track game wasn't really played much differently from the banked track version represented on *Rollergirls*.

The first team to win Montreal Roller Derby's league championship was Les Filles du Roi in 2007, known colloquially as FDR. Les Filles du Roi is a reclamation of a term originally used to describe the hundreds of women who were "recruited" by the King of France and sent to Canada, then New France, to help balance a largely male population and spark a population boom. The team wears purple and gold, the colours of the monarch, and in those early days of Canadian roller derby were notable for the glee with which they played and, especially, won. Skaters named Beater Pan-Tease and Smack Daddy stood out. Smack was a tall, striking and athletic woman with short coiffed platinum hair and a muscular jaw, who would go on to become one of the early international stars of the sport. They used to work the crowd on the straightaway at the foot of the audience, playing air guitar or dance-skating backwards. A fierce and competitive jammer named Romeo used to turn around and taunt her opponents after she broke through the pack. With names like Nameless Whorror and Not So Virgin Mary, other skaters stood out because of their sometimes absurd, sometimes playful, sometimes borderline offensive names – they'd draft a strong, aggressive skater named Hymen Danger in 2009. Yet they were lead by a quiet, comparatively conservative skater named Jess Bandit and featured an aggressive, but often smiling skater named Lil Mama. Some of the skaters were androgynous, some flaunted their femininity, one skater was a trans woman. I hadn't seen such a collection of diverse women in one place ever in my life.

In her writing, Nancy Finley points out that the roller derby skaters who drove the revival early on were not trying to bury gender or create a gender-neutral setting, pointing out that images of skulls and crossbones often have pink bows (373), for example, and that this "exaggerated conventional femininity" (374), as she calls it, disrupted the traditional, regressive patriarchal order. Roller skaters still often mimic, in a heightened way, "traditional" feminine roles in such a way as to heighten and therefore expose the absurdity of these limited, and limiting, roles of women (374). This was always on display in Montreal roller derby. Gender was never hidden as much as it was exposed, first and foremost as a construct, but eventually, and more sophisticatedly, exposed as a spectrum or as being fluid. This was a community that, for the most part, celebrated that fluidity. Finley also sees this gender complexity as a sign that the sport "is full of contradictions that cannot be oversimplified . . . The gender relations negotiated between femininities and with masculinities form a complex matrix of acquiescence, adaptation, and resistance" (383).

Most importantly to certifying its third-wave cred, women's flat track roller derby is not a women's or watered-down version of a pre-existing men's sport. Flat track roller derby, while it did emerge organically out of the older, notably coed banked track version of the game, owes very little to the traditional sports model.

It is, though, probably important to make a distinction between the older, banked track sport and the modern flat track version that has brought derby to a more prominent place than any version of the sport in its long and winding history. It would be easy to look back upon older incarnations of the game and argue that banked track roller derby was a sport built on a patriarchal model, right down to the style of play: it was aggressive, recklessly fast, very straightforward and quite simple in terms of strategy and execution. The flat track version of the game that exists now is a much more complex and cerebral game: as opposed to featuring straight-ahead speed, the flat track game rewards pace control, and it is physically positional, in that the strategy of the game supports blocking and holding as opposed to hitting and knocking down in most situations.

Perhaps most importantly, the guiding organizational philosophy of the game is "by the skaters, for the skaters." It is mandated by the sport's governing body that ownership and leadership of leagues and teams comes from within; whereas in traditional sports, for the most part, and in traditional banked track roller derby certainly, ownership and organization is top down and almost exclusively male. Even the Big Three women's sports in the country, though truly attempting to provide a female-centric sporting experience, were pushed toward conformity by the pre-established sports infrastructure they were playing upon, which was built, of course, by the men's versions of the games. The

WNBA, for example, is literally a *women's* version of the National Basketball Association.

What truly separated women's flat track roller derby from those sports was that it built its own model as it grew. That too is also what is at the heart of the difference between second-wave and third-wave feminism: the attempt to create from nothing as opposed to trying to affect change from within. In her study of DIY culture and in particular her discussion of third-wave feminist movements and their adherence to a DIY ethos, Amy Spencer further differentiates between the two waves, saying that third-wave feminism is an attempt to "take notions of feminism away from stale academic assumptions and trying to make it relevant to the lives of all women" (48).

When I first found roller derby, I immediately assumed that as a feminist, my mother – despite never really being into sports of any kind – would also "get" roller derby and love it. But despite appreciating my role in it, that has not been the case. The names in their raunch and innuendo, the uniforms and the overt, flaunted sexuality are foreign to her, even baffling. It is this almost contradictory playfulness, a sometimes seemingly ironic distance, that truly separates the late-twentieth-century waves of feminism: our foremothers were too busy getting the preliminary shit done to have time to start sports movements.

Leslie Heywood and Shari Dworkin define third-wave feminism as "a product of that contradiction between the continuation of sexism and an increasingly realizable feminist dream that today many women do have more opportunity" (41). Without earlier victories, we wouldn't live in a cultural setting that would allow for the development of a sport like flat track roller derby. Although there has been a shift toward embracing the feminist label, when I first came to the sport, my initial conclusion was that roller derby skaters were blasé about feminism. In my experience, confirmed by the experiences of most of the early feminist researchers of the game, skaters were reluctant to be labelled as a feminist, perhaps weary of what that term meant in a second-wave context. In *Hugs and Bruises*, a documentary about the founding of the league in Hamilton, one of the founding members of the Hammer City Roller Girls, Kiki, pointed out how unconscious some of that early decision making was, even in regards to what it meant for women: "I don't think that the whole empowerment of women was the catalyst behind starting the league, I think it was definitely a bi-product of it."

And actually, this distrust of past feminisms is another defining characteristic of the third-wave movement. But until we see things like expanded media coverage, a prioritization of athleticism over attractiveness and a shift in the traditional ownership model of professional sports, the relationship between roller derby, female sports in general and feminism is an essential one. Heywood and Dworkin agree and point out that "athletes need feminism because some disquieting realities persist between the pro-women's sports rhetoric and the hype" (52).

Perhaps the best way to think of it is that while the second-wave athletes were concerned with and focused on winning a battle for equality with their male counterparts, the third-wave roller derby players simply expect it.

Rollergirls was, ironically, about an isolated banked track league. Yet when the program inspired women to go on the Internet to search for information about the sport in the spring of 2006, what they ended up discovering was that there was already a movement beginning. There was already a loosely organized, grassroots system in place disseminating the rules of the game. By then, a small group of leagues committed to playing the flat track version of the game had already emerged, initially unified under the banner of the United Leagues Coalition (ULC). When women found this, found a supportive group of not only women, not only teams, but whole leagues of skaters playing a version of the game that was accessible to them, they leapt aboard. That spring and summer, they leapt aboard at an astonishing rate.

out ina bout

THE IMPORTANCE OF (AND IN)
THE LGBTQ COMMUNITY

Only twice in my life have I seen a fight in a roller derby game and they both happened in 2009. One was real and consisted of a single punch. It was at the 2009 WFTDA semifinals and Rocky Mountain was losing by a fairly large margin to the Texas Rollergirls. Late in the second half – seemingly without warning, but in the midst of a scrappy pack – DeRanged, an extraordinary skater and one of the emerging stars of the sport, suddenly reared back and punched Texas blocker Angie-Christ in the back of the head/helmet. It caused an immediate uproar in the venue, on the boutcast and in the community. DeRanged was expelled from the game and suspended for the remainder of the playoffs. Without her, her team would be upset the next day by their crosstown rivals, the Denver Roller Dolls, in the third-place game.

The other fight that I witnessed in 2009 was as far removed from the first as you could possibly get in roller derby. The combatants were smiling the whole time and the punches thrown were fake. It was late in the game in the first Clam Slam, an annual Pride Toronto Affiliate Event featuring two teams of all-queer roller derby all-stars, one with Toronto Roller Derby skaters (the Clam Diggers), the other featuring skaters from Southern Ontario, Victoria, Edmonton and Montreal (Vagine Regime Canada). Near the end of a fun, but hard-fought game at George Bell Arena in Toronto's west end, jammers Sista Fista and Bambi got tangled on turn 2 and blocker Lock N Roll jumped in to help Sista, her jammer. The skaters rolled around on the track frantically, swinging soft open-palmed slaps at each, all in good fun. Lock was smiling widely while she was escorted off the track after her expulsion.

As the derby community has evolved to be more inclusive of everyone along the gender spectrum, the name of the event has changed to reflect this, but the game has continued annually as a Pride Affiliate Event, now featuring mixed teams of North American skaters (participants have come from as far away as Indianapolis, San Francisco and Portland, Oregon). The event and the teams were inspired by an organization called the Vagine Regime. Founded in early 2008 by Injure Rogers, the Matron of Muff, the Vagine Regime (VR) is an all-queer all-star team of skaters that plays exhibition games at major events. The team has also become famous for hosting Pants Off Dance Off parties (PODOs) at big tournaments such as Philadelphia's East Coast Derby Extravaganza and annually at RollerCon in Las Vegas. The VR is an organization or support group more than an actual team with a set roster. In an interview with *Fracture Magazine* early on in the VR's history, Injure pointed out that membership was open to "anyone who's queer identified and is involved with derby . . . We invite queer, gay, lesbian, bisexual, pansexual, genderqueer, transsexual, swinger kink, etc. identified person who is involved with derby to call themselves a member" (Rogers).

From flat track roller derby's beginning, the LGBTQITSLFA communities have been a central part of the game and its community. In cities like Toronto, New York, San Francisco and Montreal, the leagues are deeply involved in events like Pride Weekend. In Toronto, for example, along with the all-star game, ToRD also has a strong presence in the Dyke March every year, and Toronto Roller Derby shirts are littered through the crowds during the Pride Parade itself. The shirts have been there since 2006, when skaters took part in the parade before the league had even officially formed. But more importantly, in small towns or less central areas, roller derby is sometimes the sole community where LGBTQ-identified women can find a support network, or a place to come out and be themselves. In this way, roller derby is political, whether it's comfortable with that role or not.

In talking about the rise of the riot grrrl within the growing DIY culture ethos of the late '90s, Amy Spencer points out that "[the riot grrrl movement] challenged the prevalent notion that girls could not have a place in political or cultural activism" (293). As an extension of this movement, flat track roller derby has hip-checked its way into cultural activism; but uniquely, it makes its statements by its very existence and by the existence of things like the ToRD's annual Pride game and the Vagine Regime.

Roller derby and sexual politics are so intertwined that it is hard to distinguish where one starts and the other ends. From the start, the political aspects of the game, though always present, never dominated the narrative that was given to the public. At least not until the Vagine Regime burst onto the scene. This approach was summed up by Paul Piche (a.k.a. Paul Bearer or "Furious" Paul Piche), an original and long-time roller derby volunteer in *Hugs and Bruises*: "[Roller Derby] has equality but it's not about equality ... It has girl power but it's not about girl power ... It's very popular in the gay community, but that's not what it's about either. Those things are just on display for everybody to enjoy and to see all those things working together and together they combined to make the awesome force that is roller derby."

Even Injure Rogers jokes about the political side of the VR, stating in that same *Fracture* interview that "[VR] started as a joke about a way to get some bootay at derby events," before turning a little more serious: "But really, it's a way for queer roller derby folks to stay connected, to support each other, and to feel like a community. Many of us, especially in small towns, don't have a lot of queer presence around us." Like the larger derby community around it, Vagine Regime started off as something purely fun and became something bigger than that.

Since 2011, I have been involved as an announcer in a small league in the east end of the Greater Toronto Area, centred in the suburbs of Oshawa, Whitby and Ajax, called Durham Region Roller Derby (DRRD). My sister, Hitz Miller, was a founding member of the league. Durham is a working-class region, built around a slowly diminishing General Motors plant. Oshawa in particular is a tough, predominantly white, conservative town that has struggled right alongside the struggles of the larger automotive industry. The roller derby league there is one of the few refuges for women outside of traditionally working-class roles, and certainly for women with any queer leanings. Those queer-identified skaters in Durham Region Roller Derby have slowly made their way to Toronto's Pride event, first as spectators, but eventually as players as well. Similarly, my first experiences with the sport in Montreal are filled with memories of the giddiness of seeing a crowd dominated by members of the LGBTQ community. Although the ratio of LGBTQ members in any given league varies by city and region, I have yet to encounter a roller derby league that doesn't embrace this aspect of its existence.

For me ToRD's annual involvement with Pride represents everything that roller derby has to offer a community. It is not simply an inclusive space, but a celebratory one, and the celebration, while being social, is also incredibly physical. It is a visceral celebration of the body, and because of its inclusiveness, it is a celebration of all that a woman's body *can* be – at whatever point along the gender spectrum that a skater may be – as opposed to traditional notions of what a woman's body *should* be. This is reflected most prevalently in ToRD's decision in 2015 to change the name of the event from the Clam Slam, which it had been called since 2009, to a rotating annual name. This was inspired by a transgender skater's criticism that the moniker Clam Slam was transmisogynistic and was causing transgender skaters to feel excluded from the event. Although trans skaters had taken part in the event from the very beginning, none had ever been involved from an organizational standpoint.

The Pride event itself, as it has risen in popularity, has begun to attract higher levels of talent and is truly an all-star game in every sense. As a one-off exhibition, it is played purely for the love of the game, and everything good about roller derby can be seen there. It is, as far as I can tell, wholly unique to the world of sports. Sure, other sports have queer versions. Softball, for example, has been a very popular sport among the lesbian community for decades, but there is no sport that at its very core is driven in large part by its relationship with the LGBTQ community. In the WFTDA's 2012 demographic survey, one in four skaters identified as lesbian, bisexual or other.

There is a fairly robust library of literature studying the relationship between sport and the LGBTQ community and it is one that universally presents a strained and even violent relationship between the two. The interwoven relationship between the foundational elements of flat track roller derby and the LGBTQ community flies in the face of everything we thought we knew about the relationship between sports and women, and sports and queer culture.

★ ★ ★

The term *homosexual* was coined in the late nineteenth century as a means by which to "pathologize same-sex love and sex as deviant" (Davison and Frank, 179). Coincidently, this pathologizing of same-sex love was occurring in the midst of the rise of both North American leisure culture and the rise of organized, competitive sport. Traditionally, sport acted as a means of reinforcing this traditional gay-straight binary (Davison and Frank, 178). At the time, the creation of this homophobia worked to "protect the privilege of a small group of men by carefully policing the membership and definition of men and masculinity" (182).

Most of the researchers in the field, including Dr. Melanie Sartore-Baldwin, a researcher in diversity-related issues in sport, seem to agree that sport, as an institution, is inherently masculine, to the point of marginalization of all other groups, and it is one that celebrates and encourages not only heterosexuality but heterosexual masculinity in particular (Sartore-Baldwin, 5). Further, Dr. Sartore-Baldwin has also argued that "the heterosexist structure of sport and sport organizations suggests that sexual stigma is not only present but also somewhat sanctioned" (7). What this has meant for gay men in sport is a life of constantly hiding their true identity. It wasn't until rugby player Gareth Thomas came out in 2009 (2) that a single gay man was identified as a professional athlete on the planet. While a few others have followed and the National Hockey

League took part in a You Can Play ad campaign encouraging gay men to play hockey, within the half-decade of Thomas' coming out, there has not been a substantial change in attitudes in men's sports.

Women have always been excluded from, or at the very least marginalized in, the sports community, queer-identifying women even more so. E. Nicole Melton, another prominent scholar of diversity and inclusion in sport, points out that "the mere presence of women in sport is seen to violate patriarchal ideals and consequently makes women the target of discrimination and stigmatization" (12). Melton, as with virtually all other scholars on the subject, points out that for women to succeed in sport they must adhere to traditional, patriarchal gender roles just to hold their tenuous space in the sports community. She concludes that "whether a woman is accepted or rejected (in sport) is particularly dependent on whether she is considered feminine or masculine, heterosexual or homosexual" (14).

Further complicating the relationship of women and sport is our sports media, which dictates the images of women in sport that are projected publicly. By focusing on women athletes' traditional femininity the sports media has glorified the athletes who adhere to these norms, reinforcing traditional sports culture (Davison and Frank, 183; Wilson, 227; Messner, 165; Chananie-Hill, Waldron and Umsted, 36), which in turn reinforces an unstated lesbian stigma (Melton, 17). This has led to a sort of celebration of women who take part in so-called traditional women's sports that highlight "beauty and grace" (Melton, 16). This is why, for example, during prime-time Olympic coverage you are more likely to see women performing synchronized swimming or gymnastics as opposed to playing basketball or field hockey (Wilson, 217; Heywood and Dworkin, 26).

This is especially demoralizing for lesbian or queer-identified women who are given the cold shoulder both by the sports they play and the media's representation of those sports and their athletes (Davison and Frank, 184; Melton, 24). This impacts women's ability to speak out about these issues for fear of either being labelled, or outted, as a lesbian and further shunned by the community (Melton, 18).

However, the group most hated in mainstream sport is undoubtedly the transgender community. Sports culture, in its rigid adherence to understanding gender as a purely binary condition, is out of step with our growing understanding of the fluidity of the gender spectrum. Different from biological sex, *gender* is seen as one's identity or internal sense of self (Melton, 13; Buzuvis, 55). *Transgender* itself is a term challenging to define and according to Erin Buzuvis, the director of the Center for Gender & Sexuality Studies at Western New England University, it has come to be an "umbrella term that may be claimed by anyone whose gender identity does not match the sex they were assigned at birth" (58).

Not only do trans people have to deal with the possibility of being singled out, they also have to deal with the reality of exclusion from sports. Testing for intersex or transgendered people has gone on for nearly as long as sport has been played competitively. Prior to 1968, when the International Olympic Committee (IOC) started to do chromosome testing, women athletes at the Olympics were subject to "visual tests" to determine their authentic sex (Buzuvis, 59).

For those who openly identify as transgender, in 2003 the IOC created a policy that allowed them to compete based on three conditions: that surgery be completed; that there be legal recognition of sex; and that hormone therapy has been undertaken (ibid., 64). While this policy seems fair and inclusive on the surface, it doesn't take much deep analysis to find some inconsistencies: in some countries getting legal recognition of a sex change may be difficult or even impossible, and many have pointed out that surgery itself is inconsequential, having no impact on athletic ability (64). Further, studies have shown that people who have transitioned (whether from male to female or vice versa) compete at the level of the sex that they have transitioned to (Epstein, 72–73).

More subtly, critics have pointed out two major problems with the IOC policy: one, it doesn't account for those who do not identify as either gender; and two, the prioritizing of masculine chromosomes and characteristics as dominant rests on the notion that men and male athletes are superior (Buzuvis, 70). Women have been excluded so long from sport that there is no way to properly compare male and female athletes in sports, but there is some evidence to suggest that given an equal playing field and equal time to evolve in certain sports, women may become equals to male athletes.

Beginning in San Francisco in 1982, the Gay Games had provided members of the LGBTQ community the best opportunity to participate in competitive athletics at an international level (Davison and Frank, 189; Symons, 91). The games have continued every four years since, but the organization has also split into two factions and the newer World OutGames now takes place a year before the Gay Games (Symons, 97). Gay Games historian Caroline Symons points out the political significance of the games as their creation marked a "shift in gay liberation from concentrating on the politics of oppression to focusing on expressing identity and pride" (88).

While this is undeniably true, the athletes at the Gay and OutGames are playing traditional sports that, outside of these events, still don't necessarily offer a safe or inclusive space. The games simply give these athletes a reprieve from oppression as opposed to actual freedom from it. Gay Games athletes surveyed by Symons and her colleagues showed that "42% suffered homophobic and verbal abuse and 46% kept their sexuality hidden from everyone in their mainstream sport club" (Symons, 105).

In her extensive work on the issue, E. Nicole Melton has identified ways that positive change can be made in sport. Specifically, she cites three key elements for creating change; namely, that to inspire change women need to

1. Create a new definition of femininity.
2. Use social media to disseminate that image.
3. Form support groups with athlete allies (other athletes, coaches, officials, etc.). (26)

Although Melton's increasing and increasingly important body of scholarly work has primarily occurred since 2010, she has yet to train her critical eye on roller derby. If she were to do so, she would see that since its birth, women's flat track roller derby has made it its singular purpose to live those three criteria that she has laid out.

Although inspired by the riot grrrls of the '90s, and tipping their helmets to some of banked track roller derby's more flamboyant stars like Ann Calvello, the twenty-first century roller derby skaters have created their own definition of what a woman is and how a woman should be. While it is up to leagues to create their own gender policies – some, such as the one in Madison,

Wisconsin, are incredibly inclusive[5] – the WFTDA itself has made strides to be more inclusive, or – more accurately – less *ex*clusive. In a "Statement About Gender" press release from November 2015, the association's official stance was laid out: "An individual who identifies as a trans woman, intersex woman, and/or gender expansive may skate with a WFTDA charter team if women's flat track roller derby is the version and composition of roller derby with which they most closely identify" ("WFTDA Broadens Protections for Athlete Gender Identity"). Although always comparatively progressive, the WFTDA's first gender policy from 2011 had become somewhat dated. Initially, the organization required skaters to identify as a woman and even went as far as to demand a note from a doctor confirming that "the athlete's sex hormones are within the medically acceptable range for a female" ("WFTDA Adopts Gender Policy"). The most abrupt shift in policy outlined in the 2015 declaration was in the decision to not require skaters to identify as women, concluding that "the gender identity of any and all WFTDA participants is considered confidential and private" ("WFTDA Broadens Protections ...").

Interestingly enough, the WFTDA-affiliated Men's Roller Derby Association (MRDA) was ahead of the WFTDA in this regard, and has never had a specific gender policy, but instead has a non-discrimination policy that states it doesn't discriminate based on gender or gender expression, among other things. The policy also states that the MRDA "does not and will not set minimum standards of masculinity for its membership or interfere with the privacy of its members" ("MRDA Non-Discrimination Policy"). This means, essentially, that anyone along the gender spectrum can play men's roller derby.

Secondly, having evolved exclusively in the social media era, flat track roller derby has always relied on social media to spread. The "by the skater; for the skater" mantra at the heart of flat track roller derby has meant that from the start, skaters eschewed any notions of being followed by mainstream sports media – and indeed pushed it away. While mainstream media has slowly started to come around to flat track roller derby, the sport has never relied upon its support and instead has created its own methods of media distribution. Teams and leagues rely as much on Twitter and Facebook team pages as they do websites, and in terms of reporting and even broadcasting games and events, it has nearly all been done internally through organizations like the Derby News Network, Canuck Derby TV and blogs like my own (derbynerd.com), and now WFTDA.tv.

Finally, Melton's mention of finding allies as support is also a key element of roller derby. For its very existence, roller derby relies on allies to function. Outside of the skaters on the track, a roller derby game requires seven on-skates officials and a minimum of ten non-skating officials (NSOs), not to mention front-of-house ticket takers, people working the vendor booths, announcers, producers, camera operators, the list goes on. The DIY ethic at its core means that roller derby cannot function without allies.

At the 2014 Quad City Chaos, the annual tournament hosted by ToRD, all of these elements were at work. I was part of the announcer crew for layer9.ca and Canuck Derby TV's broadcast of the tournament. A team from Columbus, Ohio, was playing and their coach made a request to announcers: that one of the team's skaters, the Smacktivist, a popular and very well-known athlete in the community, preferred the genderless plural pronoun *they*. The announcers never questioned the request and made every effort to use the pronoun. By the end of the weekend, it had become a norm on the tournament's broadcast. By the end of the 2014 season, the *they* pronoun had already become common in the lexicon of flat track roller derby announcers and was used for anyone else who preferred it in the playoff broadcasts on WFTDA.tv.

It's remarkable that in such a short period of time – six months – the use of a genderless pronoun was a fully integrated aspect of the sport of flat track roller derby. Within another year, by the 2015 playoffs, the announcers' tournament sourcebooks had a column for preferred pronouns that teams could fill out.

★ ★ ★

In 2014, the world came to Toronto to celebrate the first-ever WorldPride held on North American soil. It meant an increased focus and increased participation, but it also meant an increased awareness of what life is like for members of the LGBTQ community outside of Canada.

Arguably, the most moving event at WorldPride was a mass wedding performed at Toronto's popular tourist destination Casa Loma on Thursday, June 26. Featuring nearly one hundred twenty couples from around the world, many were from countries where same-sex marriage is still not allowed. What was most shocking was that many participants were from wealthy, developed countries like Australia and South Korea.

Across the city in Ted Reeve Community Arena, at the same time that this remarkable wedding was happening, representatives from sixteen North American roller derby leagues were taking part in the sixth annual Pride Affiliate all-star roller derby bout run through a collaboration between Toronto Roller Derby and the Greater Toronto Area Rollergirls. In 2014, however, there was a very special guest on hand to blow the opening whistle of the second and final game of the evening: Peaches. Her appearance was part of a week-long collaboration with Toronto Roller Derby that would culminate in her headlining WorldPride concert that would feature skaters on the stage with her throughout.

Now an international phenomenon, Peaches has been a growing icon in the LGBTQ community since her first album, *The Teaches of Peaches*, was released in 2000. It has never seemed strange to me that the rise of Peaches' career has coincided with the rise of flat track roller derby. Both, to me, are absolutely essential aspects of North American life in the twenty-first century, and both are intricately intertwined with the LGBTQ community as well.

Along with her recording career, Peaches has also made some movies, most notably the "electro rock opera" *Peaches Does Herself*. A sort of psychedelic memoir, it begins as a kind of portrait of the artist as a young woman in which the audience is introduced to a mythologized version of Peaches' creation. It is, throughout, a celebration of the female body and a stylized romp through a woman's sexual awakening and then experience. Through this process, the film also lays bare the constructed nature of human gender and sexuality; then defies those constraints as the film becomes more surreal and the desires and gender of the characters become more fluid. I was at the world premiere of *Peaches Does Herself*, and I remember leaving the Bloor Hot Docs Cinema in Toronto that night convinced that Peaches was the most important woman in the world. She represented the avant-garde of female identity in the twenty-first century: a super-empowered, hypersexual being who celebrated her body – all bodies! – with a wild glee. She was, to put it simply, free to explore how she wanted to be a woman.

And I could – and have – said the same about women's flat track roller derby. Here's a competitive game built and shaped by women in the midst of a sporting environment absolutely dominated by men. Here's a game that has not only welcomed the LGBTQ community but celebrates it, has put it at the core of its growth and has allowed it to shape the nature and attitude of the game. Here's a sport that has eschewed all traditional notions of what a sport is and how it should be, taken a punk-rock DIY approach and made it work on a national, then cross-border and now global scale. Roller derby, like Peaches, has become a twenty-first century force of nature. And I think our world is a better place for it.

the *whip it bump*

WEB STREAMING, MAINSTREAM MEDIA
AND THE SPREAD OF THE SPORT

Growing up we knew him simply as Rick the Temp.

For Canadians of a certain age, Rick Campanelli got the job that every teenager in the country wanted. In 1994, "Canada's MTV," MuchMusic, was arguably at the height of its popularity. Riding the coattails of the rise of grunge that had every teenager tuned into it for the latest music video, the company held its first MuchTemp contest where any regular viewer in the country had a chance to become an on-air temp at the TV station. Although twenty-four at the time, Campanelli looked much younger and when he got the job, I, like many other young Canadians, hated him. We used to make fun of him, criticize his approach, abilities, the way he dressed, all purely from jealousy because in reality he was fine and did better than we all would have done. But it wasn't personal, and we would have reacted the same toward anyone else. Although we would never admit it, we all wanted to be Rick the Temp.

Campanelli has become a well-known face in Canadian entertainment since that time, becoming a co-host of *ET Canada* in 2005. Eventually my jealousy toward him faded away and he became just another glossy face in the entertainment media crowd.

Fast-forward to October 2009, when the twenty-first century roller derby revival was about to get its biggest mainstream boost yet. If A&E's *Rollergirls* had started the revival, then Drew Barrymore's Hollywood film *Whip It* was about to bring it to the next level. The film was set to debut at the Toronto International Film Festival and the filmmakers had reached out to Toronto Roller Derby to help with promotion. A half-dozen skaters, Dawson included, were selected to play the Hurl Scouts, the "good" team in the movie featuring the characters played by Drew Barrymore, Kristen Wiig and Ellen Page. These pseudo Hurl Scouts were everywhere during the festival, skating the streets of downtown Toronto promoting the movie, the sport of flat track roller derby and their own league.

The film studio also worked with TIFF and the City of Toronto to turn the central Yonge-Dundas Square into an outdoor roller derby venue that would act as the "red carpet" for the stars of the film, and would also feature a roller derby game made up of the skaters from ToRD playing on two all-star teams. The track was surrounded by thousands of film fans hours before the red carpet portion of the evening with many sitting in bleachers that had been set up along the straightaway. It was easily the greatest stage for the revival of the game that we'd had yet in Canada. The impact was immense.

I was immersed enough in the game that I was able to get a great spot in the bleachers, but would not be involved in any other way. The studio had brought in announcers for the in-game play-by-play, including one of the first announcers in the revival, Chicago's Val Capone, one of my early announcer-heroes.

But acting as the MC for the evening was none other than Rick Campanelli.

Fifteen years after he had first piqued my adolescent angst, I was once again jealous of Rick the Temp.

The debut of *Whip It*, which went on to be a modest success as a movie, was one of the most important moments in roller derby's revival. Interestingly, just as television's *Rollergirls* focused on a banked track league, *Whip It* also looked to Austin's banked track TXRD Lonestar Rollergirls for inspiration. While it did get the spirit of the revival right, the sport was not quite the one that most people were playing. The film, based on a novel by Shauna Cross, also followed a similar narrative as its TV counterpart: the naive, shy rookie incredulously discovers the sport, becomes a jammer and eventually finds herself through the process – becomes "her own hero" in the words of the film. This is *the* narrative of the early part of the revival, that capturing of the moment of discovery that turns into a calling.

As the film rolled out on global screens through the rest of winter 2009/10, women flocked to the sport. There was an immediate rise in attendance at leagues all over North America that continued even as the film was released on DVD. During ToRD's 2010 season, the league regularly sold out its thousand-fan venue north of the city; for two seasons, the lineup for last-minute tickets to the Battle for the Boot, the league's championship game, extended around the building and people had to be turned away.

Whip It can also be credited for the insane rise of participation in flat track roller derby during the 2010 season. To put it in perspective, in the years leading up to the *Whip It* release, ToRD often had ten to twenty women come out for Fresh Meat, the introductory ten-week training course that skaters must complete before being eligible to play. In January 2011, when ToRD opened its doors for a "meat" and greet, there were hundreds of women waiting. Ninety of them would actually stick around to go through the program. I should point out that it wasn't all women in this fresh meat intake: there were three men in the group as well, two of whom had intentions of becoming referees, the other guy was me.

Other films had had a big impact on the revival, but not in as mainstream a way. Two documentaries in particular became must-watches for all newly converted derby players and fans: *Hell on Wheels* and *Blood on the Flat Track*. *Hell on Wheels* told the story of the earliest days of the revival and most importantly captured the moment when the flat trackers break off from the rest of the women to do their own thing. It is such an important film that Montreal Roller Derby organized a viewing of it for the Friday night of the first Beast of the East in 2008 as a kind of history lesson.

Blood on the Flat Track, directed by Lacey Leavitt and Lainy Bagwell, was released shortly after *Hell on Wheels* and acts as a sort of sequel, tracing the rise of one of the first, and most successful, flat track roller derby leagues, Seattle's Rat City Rollergirls. While *Wheels* focused on that murky birth of a game, *Blood* looked at the first few years of a league's operation and what goes into building a roller derby league. In terms of the larger derby timeline, the film picks up right where its predecessor left off in 2004. The film follows Rat's development from a tiny, fun organization playing in makeshift venues, to a big-arena sports league playing in the city's KeyArena and pulling in upward of six thousand fans a game. It also traces the early national organization of flat track roller derby through Seattle's part in the formation of the WFTDA and as eventual participants in the first WFTDA National Championship, the 2006 Dust Devil Invitational.

There have been a few other full-length docs since those two came out, with two arguably rising above the others in terms of style, substance and ability to transcend the game: 2012's *Derby Baby!: A Story of Love, Addiction and Rink Rash* and *Derby Crazy Love* in 2013. While these early film and TV projects were major players in flat track roller derby's rise, mainstream media – from 2003 to 2015 anyway – has mostly stayed away from derby. Though it could be said that flat track roller derby has stayed away from mainstream media.

Traditional banked track roller derby, which had always been run with a top-down approach as opposed to a grassroots one, had a nearly obsessive relationship with television. After its televised debut in November 1948, the sport relied upon television both for revenue and advertising. So central was television's role that the rise and fall of the game in the '50s, '60s and '70s was directly related to its relationship with the networks. This led to a need to build a flashy consumer product to maintain adequate ratings, never allowing the Seltzers time to develop roller derby as a sustainable sport, despite Leo's continued insistence that roller derby could someday be in the Olympics.

Flat track roller derby, on the other hand, has had a nearly antagonistic relationship with television. Roller derby's past relationship with TV meant that it always had to mould itself to fit as a televised consumer product, which inadvertently kept the emphasis on spectacle rather than sport. Flat track roller derby has tried to both shrug off the stigmas of the past and also develop the game into a true sport, vehemently attempting to avoid any notion of spectacle. At the competitive level, it has worked; even the fishnets of the first few years of the revival are gone. Staying away from TV for the first decade of its existence has allowed flat track roller derby to develop as a sport at a reasonable pace, has allowed it the opportunity for slow evolution and strategic experimentation, all without having to cater to the demands of a network. This distance from the media and its relative obscurity allowed the sport to go through its early growing pains as the rules were developed without too much mainstream fanfare.

Flat track roller derby's resistance toward mainstream media is built into the sport's DNA. Discussing the riot grrrl movement's discomfort with mainstream representation of women, Amy Spencer notes that "the riot grrrl scene was always wary of any media interest, sensing that their actions would be distorted by the mainstream press and that they would be represented as hysterical women" (50). As a direct descendent or expression of the riot grrrl movement, flat track derby shared the same fears. The earliest interest in the revival from media had always come with the baggage of the past. First, it was never sports journalists who went to cover roller derby, but usually entertainment or lifestyle reporters. News reports and profiles usually framed the story around the shocking discovery that the spectacle had become a sport, but it didn't really shift the spotlight away from the spectacle. Certainly in the early development of flat track roller derby, there was no interest from major sports networks like ESPN or TSN in covering it.

So, as it did with all things, when it came to covering the sport in the earliest stages of its development, the roller derby community did it itself.

The DIY approach of flat track roller derby extends well beyond league building and organization and right to the ever-expanding media community that has built up around it. This organic growth of coverage is also in line with the sport's bottom-up development focus. This build-from-the-bottom approach to roller derby coverage means that just as the leagues were setting precedents in terms of infrastructure, roller derby media was also finding new and unique ways to report on the sport, focusing nearly exclusively on live web streaming as a way of avoiding the traditional television model. In Canada, the first live web-streamed event was the 2010 Beast of the East in Montreal, and although I had little to do with the nuts and bolts of it, my voice was right smack dab in the middle of it.

By April 2010, I had started my blog at derbynerd.com and had begun to write recaps, previews and profiles and do very basic statistical analysis of the flat track game, all with a purely sports approach. Inspired by what I'd seen from the Derby News Network and from what I saw as a positive shift toward a more competitive, strategy-heavy sport than we'd ever seen from roller derby before, I dived in with an unabashedly earnest, hard-sports approach to the game. Without anything like it in Canada, people actually starting paying attention, first in Toronto, but eventually across Canada as well. I was writing for a knowledgeable reader though, not a layperson, and there wasn't yet a big market in Canada for that sort of thing. So while I didn't have many readers, those I did have were devoted.

By April 2010, along with Dawson and a videographer named Roger Foley, I'd helped start ToRD.TV, a website devoted to interviews and features about Toronto Roller Derby. We'd started things off with some rough coverage of a game between Toronto and Ottawa's Rideau Valley Roller Girls that kicked off the season where I did my first interviews with skaters. We continued through the beginning of ToRD's house league season. Most importantly, Roger would film full games and we would go to his apartment on Friday afternoons and lay down play-by-play and colour commentary tracks overtop the footage. These recording sessions happened on a few Fridays in March and April and would prove to be valuable practice. I'd watched enough sports in my life to know what a play-call should sound like, but in roller derby the vocabulary hadn't fully been developed at this point, the rhythms and timings of a game call had yet to be mapped out. DNN's coverage of the WFTDA playoffs the previous fall was the only sports-inspired calls I'd ever heard of roller derby, and they'd been essentially making it up as they went along. So Roger and I had a lot of liberating freedom to do what we thought was best. It was exhilarating to be doing something that few people had ever even tried, but in Roger's apartment it was also safe as we had the privilege of cutting, re-listening and re-recording.

While Roger and I were tinkering in Toronto, in Montreal recently retired house-league coach Dr. Johnny Capote (a.k.a. Mike Richard) was in conversation with DNN's Hurt Reynolds about how the fledgling network was producing its live-stream broadcasts with the thought of bringing something similar to Canada.

In the mid 2000s, a few sites were beginning to pop up that offered hosting space for live web streams; namely, Justin.TV and Ustream. The idea was to use one of these hosting sites as the online and viewer infrastructure so that all you would have to do was produce the content and get it on the web. It had never been easier to broadcast live events before.

When I walked into Montreal's Arena Saint-Louis early Saturday morning for the 2010 Beast of the East, I had no idea that I would be a central part of the first live webcast of Canadian flat track roller derby. While I may not have known what was up for me that weekend, Johnny Capote certainly did. At the top of the steps, near the centre of the track, Johnny had set up a broadcast "station": a table, a few laptops, a lot of wires and a whole lotta duct tape. He was working with Gilbert G., a boyfriend of the one of the skaters, to try to hold the whole thing together and

Ricky Balboa, a bench coach for Montreal's Les Contrabanditas, was plugging in a camera.

Looks interesting, I remember thinking to myself.

Noting my arrival, Johnny approached me and put a mic in my hand. I don't remember exactly what he said, but I think his coaching was something along the lines of "watch the game and talk about it." Suddenly those Friday afternoons at Roger's apartment seemed to be time exceptionally well spent. We boutcast all twenty-seven twenty-minute games that weekend and I ended up on the mic for twenty-two of them. It was very, very simple: a single overhead camera tracking the action below and sometimes just one voice; we did eventually manage to get a second mic set up at some point. But with thirteen of the sixteen teams in the tournament from outside of Montreal, people were appreciative and, more importantly, they actually watched.

"Derby time" is a funny thing. When I think back on these moments, they seem like ancient history. It seemed as if we were late to the broadcasting game in Canada, but I forget that DNN had only been producing full boutcasts for a year at that point.

The Derby News Network formed in 2007 when a bunch of the earliest derby nerds pooled their resources to form a news team. Justice Feelgood Marshall had been writing recaps for over a year at that point and had begun to compile them into a blog, the original DNN. Hurt Reynolds was also a blogger, and his Have Derby Will Travel blog chronicled his journeys across Canada and the US volunteering for leagues as they popped up during 2006 and 2007. It was an important look at the early stirrings of derby. The third key participant, Gnosis, had started a proper website called leadjammer.com and was skilled in site development. Late in 2007 the three merged forces and launched the Derby News Network in the summer of 2008.

Providing traditional sports coverage through previews, re-caps, quarterly power rankings and textcasts of games – real-time, descriptive text updates – the Derby News Network shaped the way people watched and experienced roller derby. By the 2008 WFTDA playoffs, the crew pointed a camera at the track and sent the image through the web, complementing their textcasts. For the first time ever, the top flat track roller derby being played and the best players in the game could be seen by anyone with Internet access. They continued to tinker with the set up and by the time of the 2009 playoffs, were ready for a full boutcast. Pop-ular early announcers Val Capone and Dumptruck, who is more widely known as the voice of Harley-Davidson, became derby famous during that 2009 run, and their approach to calling the game would influence all who followed.

Back in Canada, after we'd launched Canadian derby onto the Web in the summer of 2010, Johnny Capote branded his fledg-ling web-streaming site Canuck Derby TV. He began to webcast games from Montreal with a makeshift soundboard built into an old guitar case; found, or built, equipment; and rolls upon rolls of duct tape. He covered house league games generally, but also Montreal's WFTDA home games as well, and that first sum-mer both Dutchland and Boston came to town. I made the trek to call that all-important Boston-Montreal game – a burgeoning rivalry that would eventually help propel Montreal to the top of the sport.

As DNN and Canuck Derby TV began to show more and more derby, the sport was, naturally, being accessed by more and more people. By the time of the release of *Whip It* in fall 2009, people could already tune in to DNN to see what the game looked like. As the sport grew during the 2010 and '11 seasons and the number of leagues increased, these streaming services became important tools for not only learning the game, but also for charting the quickly evolving strategies of the sport. For many, the first time they would ever see the "trapping" and slow-derby strategies that arose between 2010 and 2011 would be on the webstreams. As the two networks continued to grow and improve the quality of the broadcasts, more people tuned in.

Johnny Capote quickly followed DNN's lead and began to take Canuck Derby TV on the road. He came to Toronto for the 2011 Quad City Chaos; he went to Ottawa to shoot the first Canadian Women's Roller Derby Association (CWRDA) Championship tournament and by the time of the 2011 *Blood & Thunder* Roller Derby World Cup, he joined forces with Hurt Reynolds and DNN to produce the broadcast of the first international roller derby world championship.

Soon people all around the derby community started to produce boutcasts themselves. In Vancouver, sports videographer Aaron Johnston started AMJ Productions and promptly merged with Canuck Derby TV; other groups formed in the US as well. But as the sport became bigger, and the WFTDA playoffs in particular became more popular among the roller derby community, the WFTDA itself got in on the action. Teaming up with a video production company out of Portland, Oregon, called Blaze Streaming Media, the association began to produce high-quality bout footage and launched WFTDA.tv in 2012. This became the official broadcaster of the WFTDA playoffs, along with covering major tournaments and games throughout the regular season as well.

Since 2012, the ever-growing list of flat track roller derby announcers has been unified under the Association of Flat Track Derby Announcers (AFTDA) banner, a governing body for announcers in the sport. AFTDA has provided training, a code of conduct and a certification system for the announcers that have helped to lend a professional feel to the experience. It also helped organize application processes for the major tournaments including the Big Five, the five WFTDA Division 1 playoff tournaments. I, along with a few other veteran Canadian announcers – Montreal's legendary Plastik Patrik, Lightning Slim and Captain Lou El Bammo out of Guelph and Kitchener-Waterloo – were the first Canadians to gain membership.

Announcers themselves have come a long way. Beginning as costumed trackside shills probably closer to carnival barkers than sports announcers, as the game has become more athletic and focused on sport over spectacle, so too have the announcers. Now, along with trackside announcers who act as hosts for the live audience and provide minimal play-by-play, there is a growing community of broadcast announcers who ply their trade in a more traditional manner. Increasingly divided into distinct colour and play-by-play roles, with the increased use of and access to stats (both archived and in real time), a roller derby broadcast now sounds very similar to any other sports call with the play-by-play announcer calling the action on the track and the colour commentator adding stats and analysis during breaks in gameplay.

Due to these significant changes in approach and focus, some of the game's most eccentric early announcers have slipped away or simply pulled back from the game. Toronto's original trackside announcer, Crankypants, is a good example. Mohawked, always interestingly yet impeccably dressed in traditional suits or suits of his own making, the perpetually screeching and suicide-seat prowling Cranky was a fixture at early ToRD games, imploring the crowds to get "LOUDER!" He respected the game, but prided himself more on creating atmosphere, on pumping up the fans than providing traditional play-by-play. His passion for roller derby has never waned, yet as ToRD became larger, and also more shiny and streamlined and grew away from its more local/community-feel, Cranky pulled away. He continued to call roller derby primarily for smaller community-based leagues around Ontario, in places like Sudbury, Peterborough and Alliston.

I can understand Cranky's decision. The game has changed and in the larger leagues like Toronto, Montreal and Vancouver in particular, creating a winning organization has become as important as nurturing community. Starting in 2012, I have also been one of the trackside announcers for Durham Region Roller Derby in Greater Toronto's far east. Compared to ToRD, it is a tiny league of about fifty or so women, who play competitive derby, but on a smaller, local scale. Although they have a travel team that plays periodically throughout Ontario, as of 2016 they were not affiliated with the WFTDA. There is a different feel at these games and amongst the participants: the grassroots, community-based activism at its heart is still palpable; whereas in larger leagues like ToRD, that activism is more nuanced and less obvious, the grassroots now buried deeper in the foundational underpinnings of a competitive sports organization. I value my time calling for DRRD as it reminds me of the roots of the revival with its community-based feel.

Other announcers have managed to adapt to the changes in the game and the attitude surrounding the sport and, more importantly, have maintained their enjoyment of the game at both the local and competitive levels. No announcer has managed this transition as well as Plastik Patrik.

Patrik was the first announcer I ever saw at a game and probably ruined me for announcers for a long time. An exquisite, visually hyper-feminized human – when dressed for games

– before roller derby Patrik was known primarily as a DJ and as the lead singer of the band Patrik et les Brutes. Always at the centre of the game in Montreal, Patrik at first remained largely ignorant about the larger derby community, but eventually began to travel with Montreal's colourful, incredibly competitive travel team, the New Skids on the Block. The team, along with their fans, is often called the Neon Army due to its bright, neon uniforms, which, despite becoming more streamlined and athletic over the years, have never lost the neon flare. As Patrik's travel increased and he began to shift over to broadcasting, he began to become more than just an entertaining aspect of the production and has become one of the most widely known and admired announcers in the sport. He's an important part of the WFTDA.tv's annual playoff coverage, not to mention that he eventually became a bench coach for the New Skids as well. The beautiful thing about roller derby is that Patrik has managed this transition without having to change his image. He still dresses as stunningly and evocatively as he did in those early days, although he did admit to me that he was once discouraged from wearing only a skimpy bikini on camera, but his fluently bilingual play-by-play has become taut, professional and very popular.

By 2014, the derby media landscape had shifted significantly. The Derby News Network shuttered its site in the fall of that year during the playoff season, citing collaborative and organizational issues with the WFTDA. Canuck Derby TV, unfortunately and for different reasons, followed suit. When Canuck Derby TV and AMJ Productions had merged, they produced some of the best footage of flat track roller derby we had yet seen, and had ambitiously set out to provide high-quality, well-produced multi-camera productions of the sport all across Canada. Well ahead of its time, Canuck Derby TV never found the financial backing it needed to maintain its massive production, and when AMJ pulled out of the network due to financial problems, coverage slowed considerably. But on a smaller, more manageable scale, live streaming has continued in Canada.

The largest archive of video covering the roller derby revival in Canada, and maybe the world, can be found at layer9.ca. Since Toronto Roller Derby's inception in 2007, William Clarke, known as layer9 or more commonly as Mr. Force[6], has been travelling Ontario, with many forays into the United States and even off the continent to sit trackside at turn 1. There, he has been filming single-camera footage of games, all archived on his site. Eventually, as web streaming became more common, and more important, William took over production reigns of ToRD. TV after Roger Foley left Toronto. William Clarke has slowly built up one of the most consistent game productions in flat track. Along with producing and streaming live games, layer9.ca is one of the most important archives in the sport, and includes – among many other important videos – the only remaining full-game footage from Team Canada's initial formation and the first international tour to the United Kingdom in 2008.

As the community continued to grow, mainstream media slowly began creeping around the fringes of the sport. After the 2010 WFTDA championship game in Chicago, SI.com, the website of *Sports Illustrated*, mentioned the game and profiled the skater who had scored the game-winning points, using only her real name. Shortly after that, one of the game's biggest stars, Gotham's Suzy Hotrod, was one of the featured athletes in *ESPN The Magazine*'s Body Issue, a magazine profiling some of the fittest athletes in sports. For the first time ever, major sports media had included a roller derby skater next to her counterparts in professional and Olympic sports.

In Canada, still a few years behind the States in terms of roller derby coverage and awareness, the attention has been more locally focused. CBC has provided periodic coverage across the country, such as their 2012 story on the Hammer City Roller Girls as part of their Sports Day in Canada coverage, but the most consistent coverage has come from networks in Toronto. Starting with highlights from the 2009 ToRD championship game, City TV has increasingly featured roller derby in its sports coverage. By 2012, the sports anchors were regularly recapping both travel team and house league results accompanied by highlights on their Monday sportscasts, interspersed with features and profiles. During the 2014 season, two Toronto roller derby skaters, Sneaky Dee and Dusty Watson, were featured as Toronto's Athletes of the Week on the network's dinnertime news hour.

In fall 2010, I was starting to get comfortable in my role covering the sport. I'd been writing my blog for nearly a year and had been working with ToRD.TV and Canuck Derby TV for nearly eight months and felt as if I were finding my rhythm both as a roller derby journalist and announcer when TV came calling. In addition to their major products, the Toronto-based telecommunications giant Rogers runs local-access style television stations across the province called Rogers TV. Given the massive population of the province, particularly in Toronto, production quality is quite high and includes coverage for the Toronto Marlies, the Toronto Maple Leafs' AHL affiliate. Brendan Peltier the producer of Marlies' games, was the first to approach Toronto Roller Derby about the potential of adding roller derby to its sports coverage. When the league came looking for announcers, I was the only one who had any broadcast experience at all. Teamed with ToRD skater Monichrome, on October 20 we called the 2010 Battle for the Boot on local television. It was the first time that the modern incarnation of flat track roller derby had been aired on Canadian television.

In 2011 we broadcast the semifinal in addition to the final, then beginning in 2012 regular season games began to be shown as well. Since that time, Rogers TV has expanded its local coverage across the province, covering house leagues in large cities and small towns alike. However, since it is local television and without the same pressure from sponsors, there have been no demands made upon the leagues to produce a spectacle to raise viewership. Peltier and Rogers TV have simply sat back and covered the evolution of the game. Although we do assume a less knowledgeable audience, as announcers, we have called and presented the game as we would have any sport, and as we would have on any of the roller derby–specific web-streaming sites.

Compared to some of the Seltzers' success on major US network television in the 1950s and '60s, the current roller derby broadcast community, whether the numerous web-streaming sites or Rogers' local TV broadcasts, seems modest at best. But it also seems reflective of the differences between this modern incarnation and its antecedents: compared to its flashy, spectacular past, roller derby is now closer to Olympic-style amateur sports than professional, and the muted spectacle of local-TV coverage seems appropriate.

In a direct comparison between past and present, however, Leo Seltzer's initial foray into network television led to a massive two-year boom in the growth of roller derby as a spectator sport. From 1949 to 1951 the original roller derby was never bigger. But as the newness of the sport faded and television executives began to produce more and more programming for their fledgling networks, roller derby found itself on smaller and smaller stations, until it nearly faded away.

Modern roller derby saw a similar peak-and-valley scenario after the release of *Whip It*. Two years of increased audiences across the board, followed by a quick settling back to the levels that had preceded it. A certain group of derby pundits and fans have panicked over this decrease, but they seem to be failing to see the bigger picture.

The main difference is that post *Whip It*, unlike in 1951's post-network era, the sport itself has not faded away. Indeed, it has actually continued to grow at a steady rate. While audiences in major centres are slipping, the amount of people playing roller derby in all centres has continued to rise. Unlike CBS and ABC's limited influence on the game, which never sparked a broader interest in playing, the *Whip It* bump's great legacy is in how many people it brought to play the sport. Movies like this, along with the rise in web streaming, made the sport accessible to people. That, coupled with a flat track design that could be set up anywhere there was enough space, saw women flock, not to watch the game, but to participate in it.

In 2009, pre *Whip It*, there were about seven women's flat track roller derby leagues in Ontario. By 2011 there were over twenty; by 2014 there were more than fifty women's, men's and juniors' leagues operating in the province of Ontario alone.

While in the present this means that there are more people playing and participating in the sport than there are audience members lining up to watch it, future fan bases are being built. "Derby-intelligence" is growing among an ever-expanding base of participants that will nurture a future audience that will know the game more intimately than any other has before.

So by 2014, the sport of flat track roller derby as played by those in the WFTDA had, for the most part, come of age. Strategic evolution had become very nuanced and subtle, while the previous loopholes of a once hastily written rule set were shored up. With such a strong infrastructure in place, there has been increasing, but still quite cautious, interest from mainstream media. Perhaps most notably, on ESPNW.com, a women's-sports-focused arm of the American sports media behemoth, writer Andy Frye has been writing articles about the sport since 2013. These are primarily a series of skater profiles on some of the sports' best and most well-known competitors, including Bonnie Thunders, Loren Mutch and speed skater Erin Jackson, and often have provocative titles like "Meet...the LeBron James of roller derby?" That was Bonnie, by the way. By 2015, his articles were a regular part of the build up to the WFTDA playoffs. It seemed as if the sport was on the verge of some sort of mainstream media acceptance.

Enter ESPN3.

On August 7, 2015, the WFTDA posted a press release announcing that the association had signed a contract with ESPN to air the 2015 WFTDA Championship and third-place games live on ESPN3. In the release, WFTDA Director of Broadcast Erica Vanstone, known in the community as Double H, said, "After ten years of the WFTDA bringing the highest level of derby competitions to the world, it made sense for us to collaborate with the worldwide leader in sports broadcasting." This marked a massive shift in flat track roller derby's relationship with the mainstream sports community, ending a long-held and understandable resistance. It seemed as if the sport had finally become strong enough – independent enough – to survive the encroachment of mainstream media. But shaking off that resistance has not been an easy process.

It remains to be seen what kind of influence ESPN's growing coverage of the game will have. But even it is approaching the sport slowly and modestly, beginning by showing coverage on the littlest sister in the brand, ESPN3. But the network, represented by director Ray Colaiacovo, showed an interest in working directly with the community, and the first WFTDA Championship games broadcast on the network in 2015 featured broadcasters and reporters from the community; I was honoured to be included on that broadcast team. The cautious and integrated approach seems perfectly suited for a sport that had resisted the mainstream media and in turn had been largely ignored for so long. Also, the timing for the game on the track seemed right. After a decade of steady development, by 2015 the sport seemed ready for the spotlight.

lifestyle vs. sport

MEN, CHILDREN AND THE
GRASSROOTS EXPLOSION

I don't know if nervous is the word I would use.

It was that specific mix of tension and adrenaline that I could feel sitting in the pit of my stomach, but I felt more excitement than nerves. I looked ahead to the pack of skaters who were jostling for position about ten feet in front of me. My head swivelled down to the pink start line that sat right in front of my skates. I noticed – maybe for the first time – that my skates were scuffed, broken in. A few of the laces were beginning to fray, the toe covers were tattered and the leather along the sides of them was beginning to wear. It surprised me that these tools at the end of my legs had suddenly taken on the look of proper roller skates.

The Jam Timer yelled "five seconds" and I crouched, caught off guard. I took a few settling steps on the spot. I couldn't help myself and reached up to touch the helmet cover; it was there, pulled taut over my helmet.

I risked a quick look over my right shoulder to the jammer who shared the start line with me and was startled to notice that she was looking at me. Right at me. When we locked eyes, she smiled very, very subtly. She was not nervous. There was not a mix of wrenching emotions twisting up her stomach. This was not her first jam with the star on her helmet.

The skater next to me was Getcha Kicks, a respected veteran skater and, at the time, the top jammer for the GTA Rollergirls' travel team, the G-sTARs. I was fairly well known by then as the Derby Nerd, a writer and announcer who had only recently completed Toronto Roller Derby's 2011 fresh meat training program and who was playing in his first regulation game of roller derby. It was the second half of the game, a public coed bout, and throughout the first half I'd gotten used to the fact that the roller girls in the game were relishing the opportunity to hip check the Nerd. With eight angry eyes glaring back at the star on my helmet, that helmet cover had never felt as much like a target as it did right then.

The whistle blew.

I wish I could recount in great, enlightening detail every moment of that jam, but while I will never forget the feeling of starting on that jam line, once the jam began, it all became a blur. I managed to earn lead jammer status, due as much to my blockers as to anything in particular I did, but when I went around on my scoring pass, I made the fatal new-jammer error: I didn't properly assess the location of the other jammer. When I started scoring points, GK, as she is most commonly known, was right behind me and made a pass as well, so I had to take another lap and I remember as I hit the back of the pack for the second time pounding my hips ferociously to call off the jam before GK could follow me through again. It was exhilarating and a little terrifying. But I'd done it: I'd jammed; I'd survived.

In the summer of 2011, there were virtually no men playing organized roller derby in Canada. So rare a thing was it that the closest we had to a team was a loosely constructed national team held together by the few men capable of playing that level in Montreal, Red Deer, Calgary and Vancouver. Not surprisingly, these cities were where the first Canadian men's teams were percolating at the time. The men in my coed exhibition game were all referees or coaches from the GTA Rollergirls, and they weren't particularly good. Sloppy Boggins, a Swede who was an excellent and experienced skater and had recently been named coach of the Swedish national team, was the only man on the opposing team who had caused me any worry at all. The vast majority of the women in the game were way better and way more experienced than I was, so I tried to avoid them and instead focused my attention on the other men. In particular, I remember picking on a newer referee named Harrassin' Ford who was bigger than I was, but wobbly on his skates and easy for me to knock out and drag back. I owned Ford that game.

That game would essentially represent the zenith of my roller derby playing career. I had never intended to play, I just wanted to learn the game from the inside, and I've since reserved my quads for leisurely skates along Toronto's lakeshore, while across North America that summer men were beginning to lace up to play, no longer happy to just sit back as spectators. I'm still an okay skater, but although I know the game inside and out, I don't know how comfortable I would be in a game situation. I do know that if ever I were to meet Harrassin' Ford on the track again, it would not be pretty. Thankfully, he's played so much roller derby since the summer of 2011 that he probably doesn't remember that game anyway and would spare me. In 2012, Harrassin' Ford, along with other bench coaches, managers and referees, founded Toronto Men's Roller Derby (TMRD). Later that year, Ford would be selected as the lone Toronto representative on

Team Canada and would travel to Birmingham, England, to play in the first Men's Roller Derby World Cup against fourteen other nations. All across the world, the boys had taken up the women's game.

Although it sometimes seems as if roller derby had always been a women's game, it, of course, was not. From the very beginning, Leo Seltzer's roller derby had been coed, played by alternating jams between the two sexes. Through much of the early Seltzer-era roller derby, women and men had numerical counterparts who would trade off with each other jam by jam. But though Charlie O'Connell is largely considered the greatest skater of the banked track era, it is the women who have become legendary. From Josephine "Ma" Bogash, Midge "Toughie" Brasuhn and Gerry Murray to Joanie Weston and Ann Calvello, it was always the women who provided the great draw for roller derby, and aside from the prevalence of O'Connell in the '60s, marketing for the sport reflected that.

So it didn't seem out of place when the modern revival of the sport was one orchestrated by women for women, and from about 2001 to 2007, the women had the revival all to themselves. Things started to shift after that, and once the defining year of flat track, 2009, had passed, the doors opened wide for all. Though men are leaping into the game at a pretty quick rate, the fastest growing sector of roller derby in North America is junior roller derby. But while the juniors have been welcomed into the ranks with open arms, it has been a hard road to acceptance for the men, a road still largely being travelled.

It may seem strange to equate the entry of men and children into the sport, but the beginnings of both mirror each other in timing. The connections between men's and junior derby may seem on the surface to be an accident of time, but they are an off-track side effect of the on-track evolution of the women's game. The fact of the matter is that the growth of these two aspects of the game stem from the same shift in the flat track roller derby community. Men's and junior derby were essentially given the space to emerge when flat track roller derby stopped being exclusively a lifestyle and started being a sport.

★ ★ ★

The first junior roller derby program was founded in New York in the early 1950s by Leo Seltzer when he realized that the best way to produce skilled replacement players for his adult leagues was to have them start at a young age. The junior program was formed in the midst of roller derby's first explosively successful foray onto network television when interest in it had never been higher. The organization, as with its senior counterpart at the time, was a massive success, growing at one point to nearly sixty teams in the greater New York City area (Coppage, 29). The junior roller derby program grew to such a point that it operated independently of the adult skaters and was often featured during the halftime of the matches on television. The first junior graduate to play in the senior ranks was a young woman named Nellie Montague (Coppage, 29). When interest in the sport faded in the mid '50s, so too did that first junior league.

In Canada, junior roller derby began in Edmonton and Toronto first in 2010, followed quickly by other cities. By 2014 there was junior derby in most major centres in the country but also small cities like Fredericton, New Brunswick; Whitehorse, Yukon; and even towns like Alliston, Ontario, and Grande Prairie, Alberta.

One of Canada's first junior leagues, Toronto Junior Roller Derby (TJRD), formed in May 2010 and was started by ToRD skater Lucid Lou and her daughter, BDI, with the support of other skater moms like Mouth of the South and Robber Blind. Within a year they had fifty young girls and boys taking part in the program and had organized the first-ever junior roller derby cross-border showdown. The TJRD Knicker Kickers hosted the Mad Misfits from Monadnock Roller Derby in Antrim, New Hampshire, at ToRD's Hangar. At the time, the juniors were playing a LOCO, or low contact, version of the WFTDA rule set. However, with the eventual development and growth of the first youth skating organization, Junior Roller Derby Association (JRDA), the youngsters eventually began to be separated by skill level (there were three levels), with the top skaters playing a virtually identical version of the game as their senior counterparts.

Stirrings of both men's and junior first began in 2007, when a junior club was formed in Tucson, Arizona, followed shortly by another in Seattle, and when men's teams were formed in Northampton, Massachusetts, and New York City. The first junior's and men's games would be played by these initial clubs before the year was out.

In April 2007, the Men's Derby Coalition was formed by the three existent teams – Baltimore's Harm City joined Northampton's Pioneer Valley Roller Derby and New York's New York Shock Exchange – and the first meeting was held as those teams hashed out ways to grow and promote the sport. New York's Jonathan R and Pioneer Valley's Bazooka Joe were two central figures in the early MDC, but one of my future derby heroes, Justice Feelgood Marshall, who was already writing about roller derby on his fledgling Derby News Network, was a key early member of Harm City.

Similarly, the Junior Roller Derby Association was formed not long after in 2009. Just as the young girls starting off in junior derby often had connections to the game through their mothers, the men involved in starting men's roller derby were almost universally insiders as well, in the form of refs, coaches, announcers or writers.

However, that is where the similarities in the development of men's and junior derby end. While junior roller derby was immediately celebrated and nurtured, the arrival of men's derby on the flat track scene was met with considerable resistance, a resistance that has never fully ended though it has certainly waned.

Flat track roller derby has benefited so much from evolving in the twenty-first century. The speed at which roller derby has grown and changed is directly tied to Internet and Web tools from the ease of video sharing to the organizational and marketing benefits provided by social media. But another positive aspect of evolving during this time is that so much of the growth of the game on and off the track has been captured on video. Just as the earliest days of the women's revival were captured in *Rollergirls*, *Blood on the Flat Track* and especially *Hell on Wheels*, the earliest days of the men's game were captured by Kat Vecchio in her documentary *This Is How I Roll*.

As with the *Hell on Wheels* filmmakers, Vecchio was present for seemingly every major route marker along the way during the first four years of men's derby, from the formation of the first teams to the development of the MDC right through to the transition to the WFTDA-affiliated Men's Roller Derby Association. She also captures, poignantly, the resistance that men faced early on, defined by the loosely organized No Balls in Derby movement that saw skaters sporting merchandise with the statement on it in silent protest. Men's roller derby, sometimes called merby, was called, derogatorily, *dangle* derby by many of its detractors. The doc features video of skaters being harassed in the middle of a game by belligerent fans who didn't seem to mind denigrating the very sport they'd paid to attend as long as there were no women on the track.

In retrospect, it is interesting to see that the first men entering the sport faced a lot of the same criticism and struggles as the women did during the initial revival. As the first women had been, those first male skaters were dismissed as non-athletes and their sport was belittled by the mainstream. However, in addition to those broad criticisms, they were also told, almost universally, that the track was too small for them, despite the flat track matching the same dimensions as the banked tracks that men had skated on without issue for decades previous. Because the modern roller derby revival had been started by women, they were often ridiculed for playing a "girl's sport." Abe Drinkin', one of the founding members of the New York Shock Exchange and a long-time manager and coach of the Gotham Girls Roller Derby, perhaps said it best during an interview in *This Is How I Roll*: "If roller derby is a fringe sport in general, then men's roller derby is the fringe of the fringe."

The biggest opposition actually came from the roller girls themselves. And no less than the game's top player, Bonnie Thunders, wearing her No Balls in Derby shirt, is interviewed in the movie openly expressing her displeasure at the men's game. Stated, and understandable, reasons for the resistance focused on the revival being a feminist lifestyle movement or flat tracks being safe spaces for women, or simply because men have other sports. Not only was there individual and personal resistance from 2007 to 2009, there was also notable organizational resistance from the WFTDA. Given the power that the skater-run governing body has, this could have easily been the death knell for the men's flat track movement.

But then everything changed in 2009.

In 2009 roller derby took its great leap forward by taking a great leap backwards. From Denver and Oly's sleek athleticism along with the decision to wear their real names on their jerseys (Denver) or none at all (Oly), to the Duke City–inspired evolution of pace-control strategies and the use of out of bounds as a viable area of the flat track playing field, flat track roller derby began its slow, sometimes awkward transition from spectacle to sport. By 2010, when attitudes inside and outside the game began to shift to reflect this change on the track, it seemed inevitable that both children and men would become part of the future. Having men play the game became as reasonable as women playing basketball or hockey: true sport knows no gender. The same, of course, holds true for children. And while acceptance is still not universal – and probably never will be, in the same way that even in the twenty-first century there are still countless men who think women shouldn't play sports like hockey or football – it has become institutional.

At the third MDC annual meeting in 2010, then WFTDA president Bloody Mary was a special guest and was set to make a speech about the WFTDA's "evolving" attitude toward the men's game. As luck would have it, Kat Vecchio's cameras were not only at the conference, but were in the room to capture the defining moment. Near the end of her speech, Bloody Mary captures the changing attitude and nature of the game quite poignantly when she announces that the WFTDA is ready to work with the men's organization, concluding that "*sport* is at the centre of what we [the WFTDA] are doing now" (my emphasis). That word choice, and that particular phrasing, says everything about how the game had changed during that brief stretch of time. The WFTDA was officially acknowledging that flat track roller derby had become something more, while also less, than a lifestyle movement; it had become a true sport.

Change and growth for the men, not to mention the juniors, has been rapid since Bloody Mary spoke at that 2010 MDC meeting. The Men's Derby Coalition, for example, became the Men's Roller Derby Association, and the first Men's Roller Derby World Cup was played in early 2014 in Birmingham, England, and featured fifteen countries, two more than in the first women's World Cup three years prior. Similarly, the juniors had their first World Cup in 2015, but it was more of a proof-of-concept run with only three participating nations. Also, with the release of the updated 2014 WFTDA rule set, all gender pronouns have been removed. Organizationally, the MRDA and the WFTDA have now merged their rules committees so that moving forward the men and women will be playing under the same rule set. In the fall of 2015, the WFTDA also announced that it was starting its own junior extension, the Junior Flat Track Derby Association (JFTDA), which almost immediately began to overtake the JRDA as the primary governing body for the sport's youth players.

Both the men and juniors saw a rapid increase in participation from 2010 to 2014. As of fall 2015, there were just over sixty leagues in the MRDA, including five in Canada: the Mont Royals (Montreal), the Glenmore Reservoir Dogs (Calgary), the Red Deer Dreadnaughts, the Vancouver Murder and Toronto Men's Roller Derby. The MRDA has been holding a championship tournament since 2010, with the first two being won by the New York Shock Exchange before the dominance of the controversial Your Mom Men's Derby (Des Moines, Iowa) began in 2012. A team consisting of hockey players, speed skaters and typical male members of the derby community, Your Mom upset St.

Louis by a single point at the 2012 MRDA championships to take home its first of three consecutive championships. St. Louis would eventually garner revenge and end the streak in 2015. Your Mom is controversial mostly because of the name, but also for stretching the Des Moines boundaries pretty far to include a wider-swath of skaters to choose from. However, the team and its supporters often point out that their team's reach is still small considering the massive geographical space that New York has to choose from, for example.

By June 2013, Your Mom was easily considered the best team in the ever-strengthening, ultra-competitive men's game. At that point they had managed to win twelve games in a row dating back to the previous year's playoffs. At that same time, the women's game was also in the midst of a dominating run by a dominating team. By that same point in the summer of '13, Gotham Girls Roller Derby had rung off a record-setting thirty-five consecutive wins, thirty-three of them in WFTDA regular season or playoff games, dating back to 2010. The season before, they had won their second consecutive WFTDA championship in dominant fashion over the 2009 champs Oly Rollers (233–130) and were easily considered the best team in the women's game: they were simply bigger, faster and stronger than any other women's team out there.

On June 16, 2013, Your Mom and Gotham, the men's and women's champions of flat track roller derby, squared off in a closed game in Gotham's practice space in New York City. It felt old school in a way, as the game was not opened to the public and there was no web stream, so derby fans waited excitedly (and impatiently) for any updates on the game. I will admit that I was hoping for Gotham. Probably a little too much, but I had seen Your Mom play at this point and had a feeling in the pit of my gut that a Gotham win would be challenging: they were every bit as fast, their footwork was every bit as exquisite. But for once the Gotham skaters were not bigger; they were not stronger.

Through social media, word leaked out that Your Mom was winning at half and a collective gasp arose from the derby community. At the conclusion of the game, it was hard to believe the score. Your Mom, 166; Gotham, 88. The MRDA champs had defeated the WFTDA champs. Your Mom Men's Derby was, at that moment in time, the best flat track team on the planet.

★ ★ ★

For the juniors, 2014 seemed to be an especially big year. There were now junior teams across the world, and the sport was growing so quickly that the JRDA had to create affiliate organizations to run things in the United Kingdom and Australia. Because of this competitive growth, the JRDA began to host regional and championship playoff tournaments for multiple levels. The growth of the competitive aspect of the youth movement means that junior roller derby has become more than just another youth-group opportunity; it has become the developing ground for the future senior competitors.

In Toronto, the GTA Rollergirls host an annual tournament called The Fresh and the Furious, a competitive double-elimination tournament specifically designed for new teams or new skaters from established leagues. For example, both Montreal and Toronto send their draft-eligible skaters who have recently completed their fresh-meat training. For the first time ever, the 2014 tournament featured four junior-level graduates on various teams, including one from Toronto, Fight of the Conchords. Throughout the rest of the summer, everyone in ToRD watched

as Fight made strides with ToRD's farm team and was then selected in the 2015 entry draft.

Interestingly enough, as with many of the first generation junior skaters, Fight is indeed the daughter of a skater. But their
parent doesn't play in ToRD; he plays for Toronto Men's Roller
Derby.

The biggest publicity for junior roller derby programs in 2014
came during the WFTDA playoffs in the form of Loren Mutch,
a twenty-two-year-old junior-graduate jammer from Portland's
Rose City Rollers who stole the hearts of the roller derby community. We all watched this young woman mature first into one
of her team's top jammers, then, during a heart-stopping run to
the WFTDA championship game, one of the best in the sport.

Although she'd played junior roller derby for four years before
graduating to the senior ranks, Mutch seemingly came from out
of nowhere to the larger community. Their attention had been
squarely focused on Rose City's primary jammer Scald Eagle, a
member of Team USA and Portland's top jammer for a few seasons, and even on the team's second jammer, Licker N Split, who
had begun her derby career playing for the Oly Rollers before
becoming an essential piece of the Rose City offence. But Loren
Mutch, who had skated as Mutch Mayhem as a junior and in her
first year and a half on Rose, came of age on the track during
the 2014 division playoffs. She lead the team in scoring in Rose
City's first playoff win over the Columbia QuadSquad, and kept
up with her more experienced counterparts throughout the rest
of the division playoffs.

By the 2014 WFTDA Championship tournament, the roller
derby world was about to be treated to the Loren Mutch show.
She was the team's dominant jammer, leading the team in scoring and lead percentage in each game through the quarterfinals,

semifinals and then to her masterful, utterly dominant performance in the championship game, where she was unstoppable against the greatest women's team on the planet and outskated the game's greatest jammer, Bonnie Thunders. Only strategic clock work by Gotham and an untimely jammer penalty to Scald Eagle kept Mutch off the track for the last few minutes of the championship game, in which Gotham was able to hold on for the three-point win to secure its fourth consecutive championship.

Mutch represents everything that has changed so quickly about roller derby in its modern revival. She will never wear fishnets on the track and is not heavily tattooed; she is not a punk rock roller girl looking to win the after-party. She is an incredibly fit young athlete who has put in the time and effort to excel at her sport. Actually the team, Portland's Rose City Rollers, who is one of the revival's most venerable leagues, is a perfect representation of what a top-level women's flat track roller derby looks like. They come in all shapes and sizes, and a smattering of colours, but are uniformly fit and built well for what they do. They wear identical uniforms from helmet to ankles. A skater's skates is another topic entirely and those are uniformly unique. Most of all, almost all of them skate under their government, or real, names. But that isn't to say that they don't have any of those flashes of colour that are so particular to the sport: Scald Eagle, a derby name, of course, always skates with her face painted (two wings in the Rose City colour of purple) and there are definitely some tattoos on the team. But mostly they are a fiercely competitive, driven team of skaters who all had to fight hard for their spot on that roster.

But they still lost the 2014 championship game because all of the same things could be said about Gotham; they were already full of bona fide stars and the most established skaters in the game. Maybe not quite as bigger or faster or stronger than they had been, but they were more experienced, they were more game ready, they were calmer in those final moments when it mattered most and absolutely controlled the final, crucial, ninety seconds of the game. The glee in jammer Bonnie Thunders' face when she tapped her hips knowing that she'd done just enough to win was captured by most of the derby photographers surrounding the track. The wily veteran may have been outskated that day for the first time in a long, long time, but she had not been outplayed.

Portland eventually was the team that took down Gotham, defeating them in the thrilling 2015 championship game that was broadcast on ESPN3, and the derby community has continued to marvel at their new star. The Loren Mutch era, and by proxy the junior-graduate era, has begun. You just got the feeling that the sport will never be the same. The kids are playing the game and they are growing up to be better than the previous generation. Better, perhaps, than we'd ever imagined.

★ ★ ★

On the track, the twenty-first century roller derby revival began where the Seltzer-era derby had left off in 1973, and it began where the various revivals in the '80s and '90s had left off as well; it began as a spectacle. But it began as a spectacle performed exclusively by women. Undeniably, flat track roller derby was born as an extension of third-wave feminism. The WFTDA mantra of "By the skater, for the skater" could just as easily have been "By women, for women." But as the twenty-first century rolls on, the battle lines for women's equality, at least in the developed world, have been redrawn. Feminism – through the dramatic, bold and aggressive third wave – is now about much more than women. In many ways, feminism has always been about more than women: it has been about gender equality. Logic dictates that the limiting, patriarchal roles imposed on women cannot be truly changed without also changing the roles of men. The lives of one cannot be changed for the better without also changing the lives of the other.

I should admit that I was also resistant toward men's roller derby when I first discovered the sport. There weren't many men playing then, but there were some, and I too initially felt the intrusion upon this women's game and in what I distinctly saw as a women's space. But then I started to understand flat track roller derby as a sport instead a lifestyle, and as a sport it couldn't limit participants. Also I started to accept that feminism was as much about men as it was about women, and in the early twenty-first century perhaps even more so. The addition of men, or the evolution of men wanting to join in on this women's game, is a success for feminism. Who knows what the future will bring, but right now, the majority of the leaders of the men's game are men who respect flat track roller derby as a women's invention, as a women's space in which they have been granted permission to play.

They are simply following the leaders, and their leaders are women.

In junior roller derby, faced with an increasing number of boys joining the ranks of leagues all across North America, the JRDA decided to let everyone skate. The JRDA has three levels of play based not on size, age or gender, but simply on skill. On the ability to play the sport. It remains to be seen if the new junior organization, the JFTDA, will maintain this structure, but based on the increasingly interwoven relationship between its parent organizations (WFTDA and MRDA) it is expected to do so. This new attitude toward skill-based separation is reflected in the expansive growth of the game as a community-driven grassroots sports movement, the kind of foundation that drives every sport.

So it's not surprising then, that the initial fractious gender divide seen at the adult level has never happened in as widespread a way in the junior ranks. The inaugural Junior Roller Derby Association's World Cup in 2015 did not feature boys' or girls' rosters. It featured exclusively coed national teams. It was not an event that ignored gender exactly, but it was one that accepted them as equal. The junior game is, undeniably, still a sport dominated by girls, but they have let in the boys and they have accepted them as teammates, league mates, as equal partners in growing this beautiful and beautifully inclusive game.

nerding out

THE NERD'S FIVE FAVOURITE
CANADIAN SKATERS

I need to preface this by disclosing a few things, so as to make clear the nature of my decisions in regards to this list. There is an obvious Eastern bias to this list. I'm sorry Western Canada: but I don't get to see your skaters enough to develop favourites, so that's why I made sure to call this *favourite* and not *important*.

If you were to ask me who the most important skaters were I would think of it like this: if there were a Canadian roller derby hall of fame, who would I induct? From all accounts, the top of the list from the Seltzer-era roller derby would undoubtedly be Ivy King ('30s and '40s) and Francine Cochu ('60s and '70s). In terms of the revival I'd start with skaters who are retired and would be considered "builders" of the game. It would include early skaters and retailers like RollerGirl (Lisa Suggitt), Georgia W. Tush and Kandy Barr (a.k.a. RollerBug), just for the influence they had on the early leagues. But this list would also include the country's first on-track leaders as well, skaters who had massive impact and then disappeared before their labour bore fruits, skaters like Mach Wheels and Brim Stone in Toronto, who had such an influence on skating (the former) and on travel team organization (the latter). Also, in terms of on-track leadership, a non-retired skater who didn't make my favourite list but would be a lock as a first-ballot hall of famer would be Terminal City and Team Canada's Kim "8Mean Wheeler" MacKenzie – the only skater to be a member of Canada's three national teams in 2008, '11 and '14.

I should also note that as a fan of the game outside of the country, I obviously have favourites who are not Canadian. Initially, I was mesmerized by the Oly Roller's Sassy, who controlled the game from the front of the pack like an old-school pivot, but from November 2012, when I first saw her play in person, to the writing of this book, my favourite skater in the sport has been Shaina Serelson, a super-smart Team USA blocker who began her club career in Denver before transferring to play for Portland's Rose City Rollers' Wheels of Justice, and then Melbourne's Victorian Roller Derby League for the 2016 season.

So with all that in mind, here is the list of my five favourite Canadian skaters roughly in the order that I first saw them play.

1. IRON WENCH (Jammer)
Montreal Roller Derby: La Racaille (2007–2011, 2016),
New Skids on the Block (2008–2013)
Team Canada (2011)

Iron Wench is the first skater I ever noticed, and is still probably the best jammer that our country has ever produced. Small, lean, a superbly proficient skater, she was mesmerizing to watch and was one of the few dominant jammers from pre-2010 who actually seemed to thrive with the new rule set that slowed the game down, in terms of pack play, and required jammers to be tough and fearless in addition to simply fast. That being said, she was also incredibly fast and agile, but was super fit, like one long, lean muscle. In the pre-2010 days, she used to carve up packs, exploiting any looseness on the track, and post-2010, she became a master at reading defensive walls, not only finding weaknesses, but also having the ability to exploit them. This was reminiscent of Gotham jammer Bonnie Thunders, who also thrived after the rule changes, and is largely regarded as the best jammer in the sport.

Wench was arguably the first "star" that Canada produced in the contemporary revival, being an integral piece of the offence for those first Montreal teams that made waves in the WFTDA and on the Derby News Network and WFTDA.tv. She solidified her star status by becoming the key offensive player in Team Canada's impressive run through the inaugural Roller Derby World Cup in 2011, eventually being named as Team Canada's MVP. Although she initially retired from the sport in 2013, she returned in 2016 to Montreal's house league.

I first came to notice Iron Wench in 2008 while she was playing for La Racaille. She was an unstoppable force that season for her team and led them to the 2008 championship game I remember as the Celery Championship because the fans of La Racaille, who wore green and black, brought celery to the arena and waved it all game, creating a strange sea of green. Wench led her team to the championship that season and created a roller derby superfan out of me.

2. JESS "BANDIT" PATERNOSTRO
(Pivot/Blocker)

Montreal Roller Derby: Les Filles du Roi (2007 – 2011),
New Skids on the Block (2008 – Present)
Team Canada (2011, 2014)

The nemesis to Iron Wench in Montreal Roller Derby house league play – Jess starred for La Racaille's chief rivals, Les Filles du Roi – and the pivot ying to Wench's jammer yang for the mighty New Skids on the Block, Jess Bandit was the first Canadian blocker I ever watched who truly seemed to get the game in a way that was noticeable on the track. She played the early pivot-at-the-front style, reading the play, controlling the pack and acting as the last line of defence. It was a holdover from the Seltzers' banked track roller derby, when the pivots at the front of the pack could take off as jammer if necessary; in the modern game, the jammer must physically pass the star to the pivot. It was a style mastered in the US by Sassy of the Oly Rollers and mimicked by the best pivots at the time.

Jess has survived through the changes to the game, and altered her style accordingly, remaining a linchpin of the Skids' pack longer than anyone else and was one of just a handful of skaters who played for Team Canada at both the 2011 and 2014 World Cups.

It took me a while to notice how dominant a player Jess was; it took truly understanding the flat track game – knowing to watch the pack and not the jammers to understand what was happening. But it also took the game shifting from a style of hit-and-run play to a more methodical, carefully paced game for more cerebral players like Jess to start standing out.

3. NASHER THE SMASHER (Pivot/Blocker)
Toronto Roller Derby: Chicks Ahoy! (2007–2012),
CN Power (2008–2015)
Team Canada (2014)

One of the great disappointments in my roller derby fandom was when Nasher the Smasher was not only left off of Team Canada's 2011 roster, but wasn't even included on the short list. It's actually something that I've never fully gotten over.

Easily – in this Nerd's estimation – one of the great blockers in our country's history with the game, Nasher the Smasher was part of the core of a Toronto Roller Derby house league team that won three championships from 2008 to 2012, playing in four finals in those five years. Until her retirement in 2015, Nasher was also the best blocker on the first generation of CN Power, a vital piece of the team that eventually cracked the WFTDA Division 1 playoffs.

A hard-hitting blocker, strong and athletic with the intelligence to use those physical gifts properly, she, like Jess Bandit, benefited from the slowing of the game, allowing her track sense to stick out and dominate. Early in her career she was infamously penalty-prone, hovering among the league leaders in penalties from early in ToRD's history, but the elimination of minor penalties and the slowing of the game both benefited her style: a very active skater, she used to collect minor penalties for very small infractions – glancing elbows, subtle pushes to the back – actions that are no longer considered penalties. She was such an effective blocker, there was a move in Toronto that was referred to as The Nasher, where a blocker – looking the wrong way, outward on the track – seemingly leaves the inside line open for a jammer, only to close it at the last minute in a kind of ambush.

Nasher did make Team Canada in 2014, but was, I felt, under-utilized in the medal rounds, particularly in the semifinals, where Canada went with a "small" lineup and was physically dominated by England. It was an honour three years too late, but still better late than never.

4. DUSTY WATSON (a.k.a. Dust Bunny, a.k.a. DefeCaitlin) (Jammer)

Toronto Roller Derby: Gore-Gore Rollergirls (2007–2013), CN Power (2008–2014)

Team Canada (2014)

Dusty was part of one of the great duos in early Canadian derby history, a one-two punch with her enigmatic co-jammer Bambi[7] that helped anchor a Gore-Gore Rollergirls team and led them to three ToRD Championships in the league's first four seasons. They were the offensive core of CN Power for years. There are a few reasons that I picked Dusty out of so many other great jammers: consistency, scrappiness and attitude.

Dusty wasn't always the highest scoring jammer in the league, although she was usually close to the top, and did lead ToRD's house league in scoring in its first season and finished either second or third in three others. She wasn't always the fastest, but she had the heart to out-endure faster skaters; nor was she the strongest, yet she may have been the toughest. There has probably never been a more reliable jammer in Toronto Roller Derby's history.

Dusty was a key piece of CN Power's formation, serving for two seasons as its co-captain during its rise to WFTDA Division 1 play, one of the most important times in the team's history. Full disclosure, I worked with CN Power directly for a year, and then indirectly while working as bench coach for their feeder team, the Bay Street Bruisers, and from experience, I can tell you that there probably wasn't a better teammate in the game. Positive, supportive and an undeniable on-track leader through her unwavering commitment and focused work ethic, Dusty retired at the end of 2014 after leading CN Power to another playoff appearance and finally securing a spot on the national team, skating for Canada at the 2014 Roller Derby World Cup.

5. MURPHY (a.k.a. Semi Precious) (Pivot/Blocker)

Rideau Valley Roller Girls: Slaughter Daughters (2008 – 2013), Riot Squad (2014 – Present), Vixens (2010 – Present) Team Canada (2011)

Hannah Murphy is another blocker who has somehow spent her career underrated by many in the Canadian roller derby community. Although I would say that she was not underrated by anyone who played against her from 2010 to 2014, only those who had to watch her from afar. Short-listed for both the 2011 and 2014 national teams, she eventually cracked the 2011 roster as an injury replacement, only to be one of the team's most effective and reliable blockers in the tournament. Despite that, she was left off of the final 2014 national team roster.

From 2011 to 2013 Murphy was the best blocker on the best house league team in the country, the Slaughter Daughters, appearing in three-straight Beast of the East finals, and winning two. At the same time she was helping to build the Rideau Valley Vixens into a powerhouse travel team, including leading the squad to the WFTDA Division 2 championship game in 2014, the first non-US team to advance all the way to either divisions' final game, and then the Division 1 playoffs in the following year.

Interestingly, perhaps the best example of her excellence is the depth and quality of the Rideau Valley packs that have built up around her. Despite living in Ottawa, a smallish city with three distinct roller derby leagues, the quality of play in RVRG has remain unchanged or even increased over time, a testament to Murphy's on-track leadership. While the team and league has struggled somewhat to remain competitive at the Division 1 level, skater-for-skater the league has produced some of the best blockers in the country – Reyes and Brennan come to mind. Murphy was also part of the Vixens' push to use their real names on their jerseys, and were the first Canadian travel team to have a majority of its members commit to this.

real uniforms, real names, real sport
THE SERIOUSING OF ROLLER DERBY

I'm part of the problem. Not a big part, really, but part of the problem nonetheless. In the five-year period from 2009 to 2014 flat track roller derby got really serious. The uniforms, the names, the way the sport was covered and presented all went through a massive overhaul. In one half decade the skaters went from donning fishnets and tutus to sporting Lycra and moisture-wicking polyester, and those same uniforms that once sported names like Surgical Strike, Buffy Sainte Fury and DefeCaitlin now read Hughes, Harvey and Watson. Some announcers, equally costumed, used to stumble around the track, sometimes half in the bag, imploring the audience to get belligerent. Now they are certified by the Association of Flat Track Derby Announcers (AFTDA) and have access to real-time stats to provide in-depth analysis.

On Halloween 2014 in Toronto, a skater wore a police uniform with the acronym WFTDA printed on the back and went to a party as the "fun police."

But of course, the biggest change in the seriousing of roller derby occurred on the track. Up until 2009, every version of roller derby had promoted a game of speed and violence that was often stylized, if not completely fake. Given the nature of the game, the skaters were always athletic competitors who trained hard and played harder, but some versions of the game weren't exactly competitive.

From 2009 on, the flat track game went from being a game of speed and violence to one of pace and patience. Controlling the pace, whether fast or slow, became more important than simply having the ability to out race another team. It was a simple yet controversial shift, at least for some in the game, mostly for those playing in the US. Flat track roller derby's international revolution developed at the same time as these shifts in strategy, so the larger diaspora of the sport was not as concerned with old-school debates about playing the game exclusively at breakneck speeds: international practitioners have seen flat track roller derby for what it is.

In Canada, we managed to bridge the gap pretty well. When skaters started lacing up in 2006, it wasn't necessarily to become athletes, but they quickly realized that was going to be a part of it.

"It wasn't totally *not* athletic back then," remembers Kandy Barr (a.k.a. Alyson McMullin) about the first months of the sport in Toronto, "but it maybe wasn't the focus. We had a sense that we were doing it for fun. We would have outdoor practices and drink beer and smoke cigarettes during practice, but we never wanted to suck. We always wanted to be good. We didn't *just* want to wear skirts and look cute."

Montreal's Georgia W. Tush echoes that sentiment about the first days of Montreal derby, "It was so cool to see all of the different types of weirdos that this sport attracted. It developed a lot of rock 'n' rollers into athletes."

It was a similar story in Vancouver as well: "In the first couple of years it was really a fight," recalls Lisa Suggitt. "You had the people who were there to have fun and people there to train. At TCRG [Terminal City Rollergirls] it was decided pretty early on that we were not here to have a tea party."

Roller derby got serious in Canada pretty quickly, a side effect of jumping on board as the sport was getting serious in the US. The first all-Canadian travel-team game was played between Vancouver's Terminal City All-Stars and Edmonton's Oil City Derby Girls in June 2007, but you could say that the summer of 2008 was the first summer of competitive flat track roller derby as Toronto, Hammer City and Montreal all developed travel teams and played each other. The first competitive travel team game I saw was the first time Hammer City's Eh! Team and Montreal's newly minted New Skids on the Block squared off in June at Arena Saint-Louis in Montreal. I remember the game very clearly, but anyone familiar with today's version of the sport would hardly recognize it. First, it was three periods of twenty minutes – this variation was allowed in the WFTDA rules until 2009 – and second it was like a slow speed skating race as opposed to the physical contact sport flat track roller derby is today. Packs were hard to catch making points hard to come by, and the final score that night was an astonishingly low 58–48. The game was easily the most intense I had seen. I had been used to being in an arena during house league games where the fans may have been divided, but there was still always a sense of camaraderie among the participants. But on that night the fans in the arena and the players on the track were unified in their desire: vanquish the visitors from Ontario.

Hammer City and Vancouver's Terminal City respectively dominated the very earliest days of derby in the country. In 2008, Hammer City's Eh! Team travelled south of the border and had the pleasure of heading right into the primordial ooze of flat track roller derby by taking on the Hotrod Honeys, one of TXRG's home teams in Austin – Hammer City was nowhere near ready to challenge the TXRG travel team. They then struck up a long-standing cross-border feud with the Killamazoo Derby Darlins (from Kalamazoo, Michigan) that continues to this day. Hamilton's Eh! Team also took part in the Fall Brawl (now Spring Roll) in Fort Wayne, Indiana, a multi-day travel team pseudo-tournament. There was no actual tournament structure, just an opportunity for a whole bunch of teams to come together and play multiple games against multiple opponents. Given the amateur nature of the sport, it is a format that has remained popular.

Toronto's CN Power was also born in 2008 and would be handled by both Montreal and Hammer City early on. At the time, ToRD's focus was on its massive and thriving six-team house league.

In 2009, Terminal City hosted the first travel team tournament in the country, with the Skids the sole representative of Eastern Canadian roller derby in the event. In the final of the elimination tournament, Terminal City toppled Montreal, 66–48, to take on the mantle, at least of the time, as the top team in Canada. Montreal took the title back definitively a year later when they demolished Terminal City, Hammer City and Toronto at the inaugural Quad City Chaos.

The travel team game changed the nature of the sport, made it more focused on the competition and eventually, as that competition was brought to another level, it changed the nature, shape and structure of the individual leagues. When Montreal brought slow derby (pace derby) to Canada at Toronto's QCC 2010 and trounced the best teams in the nation with their skill, athleticism and strategy, it caused a further re-examination of the structure and development of the leagues.

Up until that point in Canada, roller derby had been for everyone. Anyone could play the game at any level, and even the travel teams reflected this. In Toronto, for example, its travel team, CN Power, was made up of anyone who was willing and able to travel, with the roster changing from game to game. It wasn't necessarily a group of the best skaters in the league, but a group of the most willing. However, when Montreal came along in 2010 and started seriously kicking everyone's ass, things changed. That's when I began my brief foray into the organizational side of the sport.

In late 2010, Toronto Roller Derby held its first-ever travel team try out. The process was led, primarily, by two key figures in the early days of Toronto and Canadian roller derby: Brim Stone, the co-captain of ToRD's house league champion Gore-Gore Rollergirls, and His Unholiness, the Reverend Ramirez, the bench coach of that team. The tryout was built around a scoring system that judged skaters' skills, and although at the time there was no a ranked scrimmage system, this also became a part of the tryout process. Already heavily involved in the coverage of the game, I was consulted as part of the final selection process.

Within a year, I had joined the travel team's bench staff, joining Bench Coach Ramirez and Bench Manager Sonic Doom. But even those positions had to be figured out at the time. Primarily, the bench coach watched the game, made strategic adjustments and dealt directly with the referees, while the bench manager's focus was on running lines, making sure the next pack and jammer were ready for the next jam. This included watching for who was playing well and who was unfocused. Because of this, the bench manager had to make hard decisions on the fly, such as who to leave on the bench in the case of a penalty. At the same time that I was learning this side of the game with Ramirez and Doom, I was also deeply involved in the development of ToRD's B-level travel team, the soon-to-be repurposed Bay Street Bruisers, which was made necessary because of the increasing separation between the skill levels of the top travel team and the house league that it was pulling from.

The travel team model, which was eventually adopted in some form or another by every competitive league in the sport, changed the nature of flat track roller derby irrevocably.

In Toronto, by 2010, the house league had been trimmed down from six to a more manageable four teams, while the other two teams had been or were about to be repurposed to fit the new league model, one that was in place by 2012. It's a structure that is mirrored by leagues all around, not only in the country, but also the world.

With some variations, ToRD's structure is a good model of the way that flat track roller derby leagues are now built; it mirrors the structures of other sports, but, out of necessity, is slightly more contained. It starts with a fresh meat training program that can take skaters from zero skating ability to able to pass the WFTDA minimum skills test. From there, successful skaters graduate to the farm team. In Toronto's case, the farm team acts as a kind of C-level travel team, and plays new or smaller leagues around Ontario. From there, skaters are drafted onto one of the four house league teams at ToRD's annual entry draft. The B-level travel team is made up of all-stars from the four house league teams. The tip of the pyramid is the charter travel team, increasingly made up of a distinct roster. Both the B- and A-level travel teams are selected through the same tryout process.

WFTDA Charter Travel Team
(CN Power)
↑
B-Travel Team
(Bay Street Bruisers)
↑
House League
(Chicks Ahoy!, Death Track Dolls, Gore-Gore Rollergirls, Smoke City Betties)
↑
Farm Team
(D-VAS: Deadly Viper Assassination Squad)
↑
Fresh Meat Training

In smaller cities or towns, the structure will be simpler, and in some places organizations drop the house league and have an A-B-C travel-team structure. What this tiered organization did was shift focus away from skating simply for the sake of skating to skating with the express purpose of one day making the top travel team and playing the game at the highest level. In a city the size of Toronto, the competition level is ramped up by having multiple leagues in and around the Greater Toronto Area, which allows skaters to try out the game at a lower level before deciding whether or not to move on to ToRD to begin the process of working their way up the ladder to the top.

But this seriousing doesn't mean derby has been lost for many players. Derby is still available for all, but it now more closely resembles other sports in that there are recreation leagues, low contact leagues and semi-competitive leagues. Even within a league like ToRD, some skaters are perfectly content to play in the house league for the duration of their careers, and some skaters even stick with the D-VAS, who play a lot of games, but don't have the pressure to win that is associated with the other teams. So roller derby for everyone still remains, but not every team or even every league is for anyone.

When the structure of the game changed, that set off a series of changes around the sport's infrastructure. Most notably, the coverage and presentation of the sport got a lot more serious to reflect this.

Walt Harris was the voice of roller derby through much of the Seltzer era, and certainly his voice was front and centre during the heyday of the '60s and early '70s. A professional broadcaster with baseball's San Francisco Giants, Harris brought a level of professionalism to the calling of roller derby that gave it a serious note. Whatever was happening on the track, he presented the game calmly and provided a sobering grounding for the sometimes crazy game.

Harris, with his serious tone and the respect with which he discussed and dissected the game, is the grandfather of the modern roller derby announcer. While announcing in the early days of the revival was part spectacle, all of that has changed. Early broadcasts were defined by the conversational style of flat track's first announcers, Val Capone and Dumptruck, and although there was a definite focus on the action on the track, there were no real roles in announcing. However, there are now clearly delineated roles in terms of play-by-play and colour commentary on streams and broadcasts. This began in 2012, though it wasn't mandated by the primary broadcaster of the modern game, WFTDA.tv, until the 2013 playoffs.

The rise of statistics, in part because of the WFTDA's relationship with stats company Rinxter, has made stats analysis a regular part of the game. I gained my initial notoriety in roller derby coverage for my development of the Jammer Quotient (JQ), a comparative stat that analyzes the value a jammer has to her team by ranking five statistical categories and synthesizing these rankings to get a single number, with the highest achievable ranking being 50. It's a fairly simple stat, but one that usually accurately distinguishes the top jammer among a limited group – during a league's regular season, for example, or over the course of a tournament.

By 2014, derby announcing had more or less been figured out. I first did both play-by-play and colour for WFTDA.tv at the Division 2 playoffs in 2014, and was impressed with all of the calls. Some announcers make good teams. Detroit's AK-40oz. (play-by-play) and Austin's Kool Aid (colour) are one of the sport's premiere teams, and the play-by-play style I have always tried to emulate was developed by a Rose City announcer named Mike Chexx, who, along with LA-based colour commentator Tara Armov, called the first ESPN-broadcast WFTDA Championship game in 2015. But I feel as if I am spoiled living where I do in such a derby-rich region as Southern Ontario and where I have had many fantastic, professionally and entertainingly delivered calls with Plastik Patrik; Mr. Whistler, primarily a ToRD venue announcer; Monichrome, who is a retired skater and was my partner on Rogers TV calls in Ontario from 2010 to 2015; and Captain Lou El Bammo and Lighting Slim, who are both prominent faces on WFTDA.tv. But also, to a lesser extent – and only because of lack of quantity, certainly not quality – with Rideau Valley's Tipsy McStaggers, and mid-Ontario's Jaxalottapus, with whom I've worked more live than on-stream calls. Jax is the busiest Canadian announcer in the business, really, and announces, and sometimes plays, with a swath of Ontario leagues including

Grey Bruce, Peterborough, Northumberland Roller Girls, Durham Region Roller Derby.

But perhaps the single biggest thing that is helping make flat track roller derby such a serious enterprise is the rise of junior derby.

In 2014, when Rose City's Loren Mutch broke through and showed the potential that a junior-trained skater can bring to the sport, she was just the beginning; the first of what will be a wave of junior graduates who will forever alter the landscape of the sport. These are skaters who have played no other game, who have the footwork and instincts born out of years of training, countless hours of track time. As they grow and their bodies develop, they will alter the shape of the sport and the nature of the game. Like Loren Mutch, they will do things we didn't think possible.

These advancements have been paralleled by more serious coverage of the sport from mainstream sources as well. While previously relegated to lifestyle sections, since about late 2011/ early 2012, mainstream sports media has begun to at least pay attention. Notably, ESPNW's Andy Frye has become somewhat of a mainstream chronicler of roller derby and, in March 2014, wrote of this seriousing: "The entertaining old roller derby ... had matured into a serious sport that demanded more than excellent skating. Top-level fitness and defensive tactics have become as important as picking a derby name. And roller derby's players have, out of necessity, transformed into elite athletes in a truly international sport" ("Grateful Men Riding the Roller Wave").

Interestingly, Frye levels the importance of strategies with the picking of derby names, which, at the highest levels, are beginning to disappear altogether. Watching skaters grapple with the use of these stage names has been one of the more interesting aspects of the seriousing of the game.

jumping through loopholes
THE EVOLUTION OF THE FLAT TRACK RULES

I have a bit of a nemesis in roller derby. He probably doesn't see it as such, and probably pays little attention to me overall, if I'm being honest. There are others in the game who have more direct and heated exchanges with him than I do. He is an American blogger who became notorious as WindyMan. He has since dropped the nickname and, in an attempt to follow the game in a more direct and less-editorial manner, started a new blog called Derby Notes. I like to think of him as the anti-Nerd.

WindyMan is a derby pundit who follows the sport closely and became known for the editorial-heavy posts on his site. But while I have devoted my derby life to chronicling the sport, aside from a few micro-level forays into working with Toronto Roller Derby on the coaching and organization of its travel teams, I have kept my distance from the inner workings of the game. Over the past few years, I have also held my tongue during many social-media debates about the state of the game, for the most part choosing to observe rather than take part.

WindyMan gets right into it all, and he has focused and re-fined his attack to be directed squarely at the WFTDA. A lot of the debate swirling around the derby community centres on the way the game is played, the way that it is evolving and how this affects the so-called fan experience. In particular there is debate about how the reliance on slower strategies and how complicated the flat track game has become is slowing the growth of the spectator sport and driving fans away.

Of course, flat track's slowing of the game is not necessarily unique. The first slowing of the sport actually occurred on the banked track in the early '60s during Charlie O'Connell's emergence as the biggest star in the game. The creation of the pivot position in 1961, which corresponded with the shortening of jams, gave teams an offensive weapon at the front of the pack, which immediately made the packs slower and much more strategic (Coppage, 69–70). These shifts were met with similar controversy at the time (71) and the game was said to resemble American football, with two "lines" battling to either free a running back/jammer or hold the player back. Interestingly enough, modern flat track roller derby – with its tight, slow-moving, scrum-like formations – is more often compared to rugby than football.

But many old-schoolers, whether from the earliest days of the flat track game or even those from the earlier versions of the sport, see flat track roller derby – especially as played by the WFTDA – as a perversion of the sport. WindyMan leads the way in this line of argument, but gets support from many places as well, including sometimes from Jerry Seltzer himself. The blogger actually gave an (in)famous lecture at RollerCon 2013[8] about just this subject: how the WFTDA is not "real" roller derby and that is why the fans are running away from the game.

The hard truth of the matter is that flat track roller derby does not have a fan base to chase away. If you want to get right down to it, roller derby does not currently have, nor has ever truly had, a fan base. Period.

This is a bold statement to make, and maybe even a controversial one. But until the roller derby community accepts this basic tenet, there will be disagreement about the future of the sport.

When I say that roller derby doesn't have a fan base, I am being a little glib. People obviously watch the sport, and since its inception there have been fans very devoted to it, and at times people have even watched the sport in large numbers, but there has never been a sustained, substantial fan base in any era of the game, despite what some would have you believe. There have been blips in popularity: namely, in the mid 1930s during the first run of the game; then in the early '50s with the first foray into network television; in the late '60s and early '70s during the second sustained run on TV; and finally from 2009 to about 2011, accounted for by the *Whip It* bump. Each of those four distinct eras had good reasons for the spike in popularity and clear reasons for the subsequent declines.

During the various heights of the Seltzer runs, the sport would often draw crowds in the tens of thousands, and would fill venerable sports venues like Comiskey Park and Madison Square Garden. But when it wasn't on TV it was often treated by the spectators as a one-off spectacle; this was true even after Leo first tried to build the idea of a league. During the whole Seltzer era teams changed often, whether it was names to reflect the region they were playing in or the players on the roster. Rules changed often as well, at least early on. During Leo's run, he used to sometimes change the rules in the middle of a game. It was like a mirror image of a real sport. Don't get me wrong, it took real, incredible athleticism to play, but in hindsight, derby's lack of staying power was not surprising; what is surprising is that there were spikes of such massive popularity at all.

Decades later, the *Whip It* bump saw a surge in popularity in the sport even greater than during any of the Seltzer-era bumps. Sure, flat track roller derby never drew twenty thousand to Madison Square Garden, but for the years directly following *Whip It* there were thousands watching in multiple venues around North America. Seattle's Rat City Rollergirls averaged over six thousand fans to KeyArena during that surge, and other centres like Austin, Minnesota and New York also saw thousands coming through their doors for events. In Toronto and Vancouver, sellouts in thousand-seat venues were the norm. Only Montreal has had an unchanging audience since 2007, seemingly unaffected by anything outside of its own sphere. But here's the issue with the surge in popularity created by flat track's "bump": it wasn't ready for it. Not even close.

Post *Whip It*, there was barely a sport to grab on to, and the game being played in 2009 hardly resembled what it would look like even two years later. People weren't flocking to the game to follow a sport anyway; they were flocking to it for the spectacle just as they had during the Seltzer era. In Seattle, people filled the arena for the house league games, leaving the much more talented travel team to play most of its games in the league's practice space, while in Minnesota they were filling the stadium for travel-team games: there was no consistency from city to city. And what those people did find was a sport going through an awkward stage of growth, coming of age, if you will. It really was awkward at times. People came expecting hot chicks in fishnets pounding the crap out of each other, and while in 2009 they did find some of that still, what they mostly found were a bunch of increasingly athletic-looking women in sports uniforms who were working hard to iron out complex strategies.

That discussion of strategy is at the heart of the internal debates about the game right now. As representative of the anti-WFTDA movement, WindyMan claims that the WFTDA has perverted the rules of roller derby. He says that the WFTDA rule book is confusing because it is written, in his words, by people who "don't understand roller derby." An attitude hard to grasp, given the thousands of women who play the game and who have developed this distinct arm of it.

He is right, in that flat track roller derby has moved far from its banked track beginnings. But that is the sole place where we find agreement. WindyMan argues that flat trackers should be playing banked track roller derby, even if on a flat surface, while I stand firmly on the side of the argument that says the banked track rule set does not work on a flat track.

Because of this, there are now two distinct arms of roller derby. The remnants of Seltzer-style roller derby still exist in the modern game, most notably in the form of the Roller Derby Coalition of Leagues (RDCL), the most organized collection of banked track leagues that still exists. They are all primarily on the west coast and they play an annual championship tournament called Battle on the Bank. RDCL remains the closest to what Seltzer roller derby eventually became in the '60s. The rules have been modified to strip away the less sporty elements of the game – there are no fights or pro-wrestling style tangles anymore – but it remains a straightforward, fast-paced game that doesn't allow for skating against direction of gameplay.

Given the incredible cost of building and housing a banked track, there are simply not a lot of leagues that can manage it on a regular basis. But it is an exciting and entertaining style of derby that manages to pay homage to the past versions of the game while at the same time offering a modern competitive version of the sport. The teams in the RDCL provide some of the finest banked track roller derby I have ever seen.

As roller derby has grown in scope and popularity, competing rule sets have arisen in the flat track world, although they have arisen almost exclusively in the United States. As of 2014, there were a few alternate rule sets being played in the US, most notably the Modern Athletic Derby Endeavor (MADE) and the rule set developed by USA Roller Sports (USARS). Both try to stay as close as possible to the banked track game. It should be noted that MADE plays the same rules whether on a banked or flat track; and although I have not had much opportunity to see it beyond a few YouTube videos, this banked track rule set seems good. However, because of that adherence to the banked track game's rules, I have often found both of those rule sets awkward to watch on the flat track, mostly because the games seem forced. The style of play conflicts with the surface being played on and is particularly awkward in that they don't use the most obvious tool in the flat track strategist's tool box: the out of bounds, that space surrounding the track that doesn't exist in the banked track game.

For me, playing banked track roller derby on a flat track is the equivalent of trying to play field hockey strategies in an ice rink: you would be doing a disservice to your surface.

The criticism often levelled at the WFTDA is that the rule set is too complex and, to reiterate, that it veers too far from "traditional" roller derby. When people refer to traditional roller derby, they usually mean the way the game was played from about 1963 to 1973. But neither was always the case. When the first official

WFTDA rule set was published in 2006, it was quite a simple document, only nine pages long and not particularly detailed, similar to the final Seltzer-era rule set, which was a sparse five pages (Deford, 207). There were some arbitrary rules, such as the start formation, that attempted to mimic the banked track game. The starting area on a flat track surface is a thirty-foot-long (nine-metre-long) stretch on the first straightaway defined by two lines: the jammer line and the pivot line. In the initial rule set pivots were told to start with their skates on the pivot line, the blockers lined up directly behind them and the jammers twenty feet (six metres) back. Aside from that there was very little direction to gameplay, and the game itself looked like what you would have seen on the banked track. There were very loose definitions about the pack, fighting was still allowed, and it actually encouraged leagues to have a halftime penalty showdown, where each team's penalty leaders would have to compete in a game of the league's choosing to get extra points for her team. Previous to the official rule set, many leagues used a penalty wheel instead of giving out penalties, where the penalized skater would spin a wheel to determine her punishment, which could be anything from having to endure spank alley, where the people lining the track could take turns spanking her as she skated, to having to put on a silly suit and dance.

That initial rule set established loose parameters for the game, but it allowed for room to grow. No one before had committed to playing derby on a flat track and so no one knew what the game was going to look like when people started having a chance to master it. Although it has seemed sluggish, the evolution has actually been quite fast.

By 2007, the start formation was loosened, the pack was broadly defined as containing skaters within twenty feet (six metres) of each other, and penalties were set for intentionally destroying the pack. Fighting was relegated to being just another major penalty, though within another year, by 2008, it would be banned outright. The rule set had nearly doubled in size within that year, but a lot of it was game parameters and specifics, moulded into the shape that the game was naturally taking. The pack definition penalties were developed to stop skaters from simply skating away from other skaters. Skaters always look for loopholes to get the competitive edge.

Over the next few years, the rule set became more and more refined, while also becoming longer and more detailed. Most of the major changes occurred in regards to pack definition, starts and penalty enforcement; namely, that there had been two levels of penalties, minors and majors, with four minors adding up to a major. I look at this quirk as training wheels: the minors helped clean up the game, taking away small things like elbow jabs and other minor impact infractions. It took until the 2013 rule set to eliminate minor penalties; thus taking off the training wheels.

Perhaps the final training wheels that need to be taken off are the existence of non-impact penalties that still see a lot of skaters heading to the penalty box for actions that had no discernable effect on the game. For example, brief momentum cuts when a skater re-enters the track illegally for sometimes only a millisecond before leaving the track again, therefore not taking advantage of the illegal action, or forearm infractions that don't actually impede skaters in any substantial way or too-strict pack destruction calls when destroying the pack was not the intention and did not actually impede game play.

Starts also eventually changed to adapt to the flat track. The arbitrary starting position was quickly loosened and then abandoned all together, but then again skaters began to find the loopholes and take advantage of them. Most of those exploitations happened because of the natural slowness of the flat track. For example, jammers were initially released only after every member of the pack had crossed the pivot line. So when teams had skaters serving time in the penalty box, the blockers would stagger their start, waiting for the last possible moment to cross. The teams with the advantage responded by finding ways to override that, and they did so by exploiting the fact that the jammer would be released if, for some seemingly unforeseeable reason, there happened to be a "no pack" situation at the start. The idea that there would be no opposing skaters within ten feet (three metres) of each other seemed impossible, until teams started to "take a knee," where they would drop to the ground and intentionally take themselves out of play. The whistle would be blown because there would be no pack and the jammer would be released. This was taken to absurd levels by some teams, such as with the "dead bug" tactics of the Rideau Valley Vixens. They got into the habit of starting jams by having their pack skaters lie on their backs with their arms and legs pulled into their bodies like a dead bug, then slowly and deliberately unfold, eventually rolling over onto all fours and standing. While this no-pack situation forced the second whistle to blow, releasing the jammer and beginning the jam, the delayed reset slowed the reformation of the pack and therefore the ability to engage (blockers couldn't block if they were not in the pack); this meant that the jammers could skate through the start untouched.

Unable to effectively counter these various start strategies consistently, the team with the pack advantage then began to start as close to the jam line as possible so to gain a better defensive position against the prematurely released jammers. There were also stalemates where both teams would simply refuse to start for various reasons – both teams had multiple players in the penalty box, for instance. Sometimes the jam would simply never start and in a few infamous instances, a full two minutes passed without anyone moving. Sound confusing? That's because it was. It was during this awkward time when critics like WindyMan began to viciously attack the game, and perhaps rightfully so, but nearly every loophole strategy that occurred during that time led to the necessary strategic and rules evolutions that can be seen today. For example, the WFTDA rule set eventually moved to a single-whistle start that released the jammers immediately, eliminating the effectiveness of the delayed- or quick-start tricks.

Perhaps the defining aspect of flat track roller derby is in the pack work; this is reflected in the specificity around defining and destroying the pack. Moving forward is not as natural an act on the flat track as it is on the banked track, and this simple fact accounts for a lot of the differences in the game. By 2009 what constituted a pack was clearly defined: the largest group of skaters containing members of both teams all within ten feet (three metres) of each other. A zone of engagement was also formed that allowed individual skaters to block within twenty feet (six metres) of the front or back of the pack.

At present the full rulebook is seventy-nine pages long, but in many ways is simpler than it ever has been. A lot of the length is in detail as opposed to an abundance of rules; actually, with the removal of minor penalties, enforcement is much more straightforward. Today's WFTDA rule book resembles the rule books of any sport: it includes track specifications, explanations of game protocols and roles (from officials through to skaters) and lays out penalties – including standardized hand signals – in as much concise detail as possible. And although critics still argue that it isn't simple enough compared to banked track rule books of old, compared to the rule books of other team sports it is actually quite pared down. The rule books of both Major League Baseball and the National Hockey League, for example, are well over two hundred fifty pages long, while the National Basketball Association's, at sixty-six pages, is the only major team sport that has a rule book as slim as flat track roller derby's.

The 2010 WFTDA Championships, which had been the most well attended to that point, occurred smack dab in the middle of flat track roller derby's most awkward growth spurt. Starts were delayed or rushed, the parade of skaters to the penalty box for minor infractions hampered the flow of the game and the slow-pack strategies were still being ironed out, leading to extended periods of time during a jam when no one moved or did anything, and it led to a number of blowouts, even at the top level. Criticism was also at its height and a group calling itself Slow Derby Sucks had formed, creating a website and T-shirts. At the 2010 tournament, they came out in full force, handing out flyers and holding up large signs in the audience. The organization said that the new changes were ruining the game and, especially, the fan experience. But even then, astute observers saw the shifts, changes and confusing moments for what they were: transitional moments in a larger evolution.

By the 2015 WFTDA Championships the rules had mostly ironed themselves out and the game looked remarkably different from the one played in 2010. The games were intense, and they were exciting. In 2014 Gotham and Rose City had played in one of the most exciting games of flat track ever, and they nearly topped it in their championship rematch in 2015, a game that also happened to be broadcast on ESPN3. As the track-side analyst for the network, I had a front-row seat to it all.

The near sellout crowd at St. Paul's Roy Wilkins Auditorium was the largest since 2010 and, by all accounts, the loudest ever to line a flat track, with the crowd heavily favouring the Portland underdogs. Near the end of the game, during a stirring Rose City comeback that saw them take a lead they would not relinquish, the crowd noise reached such a level that I struggled to hear the director, Ray Colaiacovo, through my earpiece. Scrambling to find a place to hear my end-of-game instructions, one of the technical producers rushed to my aid and guided me to a quiet hallway. Prior to the game, while hooking up my earpiece and giving me my mic, this producer had seemed a little skeptical of the undertaking and admitted to me that he had never even bothered to watch a flat track game before the weekend. But after getting my instructions late in that championship game, as I returned to the track, I saw the technical producer standing alone with his hands on his hips and a smile on his face, seemingly in awe of what was happening. As I passed him on my way back to my spot trackside, he turned and leaned toward me, "Yeah I don't know if this game has a future," he cracked, winking. "Doesn't seem like the fans are into it."

goinq global

THE ROLLER DERBY WORLD CUP AND GLOBALIZATION OF THE GAME

In these early days of roller derby's development, there are some dates etched into the minds of fans and participants as key in the sport's history. April 26, 2003, the date of the first Texas Rollergirls game in Austin under the first flat track rule set, is one of the big ones. Another is December 3, 2011, and in particular one matchup that I affectionately call The Game NOT Heard Around the World. The setting was the Bunker, home of Toronto Roller Derby, and the game was the opening match of the first-ever Women's Roller Derby World Cup. The Bunker, a massive warehouse-like space with whitewashed walls and massive pillars that the tracks had to be creatively built around, was an unlikely space to hold such an event. Yet, in early winter 2011, it was set to become one of the most recognized venues in the game.

Toronto Roller Derby had moved into the venue, just across the street from its previous home at the Hangar in Downsview Park, where they'd been since June 2009, only months before the World Cup. The move to a permanent venue, first the

Hangar, then the Bunker, was a key shift for the Toronto Roller Derby and followed three years of chasing ice-less arenas and church basements for practices, which had left individual teams fending for themselves in terms of training. Moving everyone under one roof was a very important step toward shifting to a league-centric focus and the first step toward being competitive in the WFTDA.

By the beginning of 2010, the roller derby leagues that did exist were inundated with fresh meat as a result of the release of *Whip It*. In Toronto, the timing of the move to the Hangar suddenly seemed brilliant. Ninety women registered for fresh meat, four times the usual number and it was similar elsewhere. But in towns where there had been no roller derby, there suddenly was: In Ontario it started in places like Sudbury and Timmins; in British Columbia, it was Nelson and the Kootenays.

In December 2010, the roller derby magazine *Blood & Thunder* hosted one of its travelling roller derby boot camps at the Hangar, drawing in skaters from all across Ontario and even beyond, into the east coast. It was a successful weekend topped off by an all-star scrimmage that was opened to the public. After that weekend the magazine asked Toronto Roller Derby to team up with it to put on the first-ever Women's Roller Derby World Cup the following December.

It seemed almost ludicrous at the time, to take a sport barely past its infancy and try to hold an international event, and I wondered how many countries would actually be able to take part. The answer ended up being a surprising thirteen: USA, Canada, England, Australia, Finland, Sweden, France, New Zealand, Germany, Ireland, Scotland, Brazil and Argentina. It should be noted that a few countries – namely, Argentina and Brazil – ended up sending skaters who had yet to actually play a game and even had to borrow gear; nonetheless, it was happening. Flat track roller derby was spreading around the world. And it was spreading quickly.

In the midst of the planning for the Roller Derby World Cup, Toronto Roller Derby lost the Hangar, which was taken over by Volleyball Canada to build a beach volleyball training facility. However, the landlords in Downsview Park offered a new space down the street, and just in time for the event, ToRD moved into its new home.

Fast-forward to December 3, 2011, 5:00 p.m. EST, when a sport that was just barely eight years old was about to officially become international. The hosts and one of the pre-tournament favourites for the silver medal – there was never any doubt in anyone's mind that the US would take the World Cup – Canada was set to kick off the inaugural event with a preliminary bout against France, and the Derby News Network was on hand to live stream the game. At that point in time, I was the most experienced live stream roller derby announcer in Canada. I'm not bragging; at the time I was one of the *only* announcers with live stream experience in the country. My partner for the game was one of Montreal's announcers, Single Malt Scott, and we were set for the call. It was an honour to call the game; we were excited; we felt as if we were a part of history.

Then the image streamed first with garbled sound. And then none at all. The first-ever Roller Derby World Cup game was a game that no one ever heard.

That would spark the first of many criticisms lobbied at the event: from the broadcast to the venue – at this point fans of the WFTDA were used to seeing big tournaments, like the playoffs, played in large hockey or basketball arenas, and the Bunker seemed a throwback to a time when the sport was a little less polished. DNN had not evolved much in its three years of web streaming roller derby and was still a largely duct tape-and-bubble gum set-up that crashed a few times on that opening day. It was not anywhere near prepared for the volume of viewers tuning in from around the world. But looking back now, it was probably a fitting venue to hold the first World Cup and DNN, the perfect broadcast partner: small, a little rough around the edges, but incredibly intimate. Every game on both tracks was packed solid for all four days of the event, and the energy level in the building was outstanding with fans of the games constantly just an arm's-length away from the greatest skaters in the world.

In terms of sporting events, it also wasn't that compelling, featuring blowout after blowout. Although USA's dominance was expected, they surpassed even the highest expectations, simply playing the sport at an altogether different level than anyone else. USA's 532–4 semifinal victory over a solid Australian team was still shocking, even after they had knocked teams around with ease for three days.

But it wasn't just the US that dominated. Canada similarly dominated its opponents, outscoring France, Brazil and Sweden in the preliminary rounds by a combined score of 848–50, and then crushing a pretty decent Finnish team in the quarterfinals 499–31. In the final, the host nation managed to do comparatively well against USA, holding the Americans under four hundred points and scoring more against them than all of their previous opponents combined, losing 336–33.

Not to say that there weren't some compelling games and even moments, such as an Ireland/Finland preliminary round game that came down to the wire, a Canada/England semifinal that provided the best high-level action of the tournament, the New Zealand haka performed on a derby track was a sight to behold, a slight Finland upset over Sweden in the fifth-place game was one of the most exciting and emotionally intense games I've still ever seen and the roar that shook the Bunker when Team Scotland scored a single point against the USA remains one of the most vociferous responses at a sporting event that I have ever heard. The final score was 435–1.

In the end, virtually everyone agreed that the importance of the event, like so many in the sport's early evolutionary days, extended far beyond the competition on the track: it brought the sport to a level of mainstream visibility that it had not yet achieved. Mainstream news crews from newspapers and television swarmed the Bunker, intrigued by this burgeoning sport. *The Toronto Star*, in particular, provided a lot of coverage for the event, all built around the narrative of derby's transition from spectacle to sport. The newspaper's preview was called "Roller Derby's Race for Respect" and the coverage focused on how USA skaters were skating under their real names and made a quest to discover "who is the Sidney Crosby of roller derby" until the reporter, Liam Casey, began to realize a lot of skaters outside of Canada didn't actually know who Crosby was. Casey eventually flipped the hockey superstar's name for LeBron James.[9] His take away from the event? "Women's roller derby remains an amateur sport, with a strong do-it-yourself feel that many athletes appreciate. Others, however, want to see the sport grow into a more professional version."

That also summed up the importance of the tournament. The roller derby community was getting ready to push for mainstream acceptance, hoping to nudge the competitive game toward something more professional. And it did. The American skaters, a few skating under real names for the first time, included the members of the first star system in roller derby: the passionate sisters DeRanged and Psycho Babble; the jammers Atomatrix, Suzy Hotrod and Nicole "Bonnie Thunders" Williams; the imposing blocker Sexy Slaydie. But along with these already established stars, the All-World Team, the MVPs for each nation, introduced a slew of new stars to roller derby fans, including Canada's MVPs, the wonderful Montreal jammer Iron Wench and blocker/pivot Smack Daddy, also of Montreal.[10]

Three years later, and *Blood & Thunder* hosted the second Women's Roller Derby World Cup, this time in Dallas at a much bigger and more modern facility, the Kay Bailey Hutchison Convention Center. The first three days of the event were held in a large open space that accommodated three tracks and up to seven thousand spectators spread out over those three tracks. It was stunning walking among the vendor lanes that had been built to guide the attendees through the room. It was like a roller derby city had popped up in the middle of Dallas. The final day's games were held in the Center's eight-thousand-seat arena. Everything about this World Cup was bigger, including the number of participants. In only three years, the number of countries participating in the event went from thirteen to thirty, representing all six inhabited continents. But while this event was bigger and better in every way compared to Toronto's 2011 World Cup, early on it didn't look as though it would be that much more competitive on the track.

At the 2014 Roller Derby World Cup there were still muted grumblings about the one-sided nature of some of the scores, particularly in the round-robin portion of the event where established nations like Australia (515–5 over Italy), Canada (301–23 over Denmark), England (329–50 over Ireland), Finland (312–38 over Mexico) and Sweden (459–0 over Japan) smothered their competition in mercifully shorter-than-regulation games.

But it would be hard to argue that anything else was expected in those rounds: Italy did not come into the World Cup thinking it would triumph over Australia, Denmark was probably quite content to score twenty-three points against Canada and when Puerto Rican jammer Goomba Toomba managed to score her team's only three points in a 637–3 loss to USA, the room erupted as if the team had just won the World Cup trophy itself.

It actually isn't that unprecedented in the history of sports to have initially one-sided international events. For example, in ice hockey's first forays into international competition at the 1920 and '24 Olympics, the scores were often absurd. A Canadian amateur team won its three 1924 round-robin games by a combined score of 85–0, yet hockey historians look back upon those two tournaments as being instrumental in the global growth of the sport. It's undeniable that historians will one day look back upon these initial Roller Derby World Cups with the same sort of favour. Except for the top four teams, or honestly just the second- through to fourth-place teams, winning and losing was not necessarily the number one goal. This tournament, like its predecessor, was about so much more than that.

Even Jerry Seltzer, who had been known to be publicly critical of the flat track game, seemed overwhelmed by the event. He wrote a long glowing piece about it on his blog, rollerderbyjesus. com, concluding that "what I saw was a sport that in its intrinsic honesty and participation is untouched by anything else out there, and the competitors are all sisters in the truest sense." This, of course, was an important admission, as from Transcontinental Roller Derby in the '30s to the World Skating League's RollerJam in the '90s, the Seltzer name *was* roller derby. From patriarch Leo and his brother Oscar through to Leo's son, Jerry, and daughter, Gloria, the Seltzer name had been the beating heart of the sport for seven decades before the flat track revolution brought the game to a level that transcended any one name.

It's not hard to see why Jerry was so taken by the event. In a 2010 interview at the WFTDA Championships in Chicago, Jerry pointed out that "all [his father] wanted was a legitimate game that could be in the Olympics." It never came to pass in Leo's lifetime, nor even with Jerry at the reigns, yet here it was, not the Olympics exactly, but truly global. Even if growth at that point had slowed somewhat in North America, it was a sport still very much growing on the rest of the planet.

Despite the disparity in some games, competitive growth in the sport was also evident at the second World Cup. Brazil and Argentina had been virtual doormats in 2011, but entered the 2014 event with a certain air of confidence. Winless three years prior, Brazil notched round-robin victories in tight wins over Portugal and Switzerland, and the Argentinians had a dominant performance over Denmark. Argentina then scored the upset of the World Cup in a very physical 205–143 victory over France in the Round of 16. France had finished seventh in 2011 and was expected by most to be a lock for a Top 8 finish in Dallas. Similarly, other returning nations like Ireland, Scotland and New Zealand emerged as leaders of the global game.

There was shifting in power at the top too, with England gaining revenge on a Canadian team that had topped them three years before with a hard-fought but convincing 156–112 win in the semifinals, and then Australia did so as well, taking advantage of a spent Canadian squad with a thoroughly impressive 197–128 victory in the bronze medal matchup. Finally, England shattered all expectations and won over the hearts of the world with a performance for the ages against the Americans, winning the silver medal in a 219–105 loss in the gold medal game. No national team had ever held the Americans to such a low total or managed to score so many points against them.[11]

But despite the giddiness of that result – and the fifty-four points Australia managed against the American juggernaut in the semifinals – it was still evident that USA represented the best in the world. At the conclusion of the final game in 2014, England, battered, bruised and exhausted, looked as if they'd truly left it all on the track, while the Americans – still very much bigger, faster, stronger – appeared as if they were ready to play at least another sixty minutes.

So even if the bar did not quite seem as high as it once was, it was still the Americans who were setting it.

But in terms of global growth, the most significant tournament in 2014 may have been the inaugural Men's Roller Derby World Cup held in Birmingham, England, in March of that year. Fifteen countries were represented at the Men's World Cup. Of the fifteen men's countries participating, eleven of them were represented at the first women's World Cup and the other four participated in the second in Dallas. Brazil and New Zealand were the only countries from the first two women's World Cup that didn't compete in the men's, which meant that for the most part, where the women played, the men were following suit. The results were, not surprisingly, similar to those of the women's tournaments. Although France nudged Australia to slip into the Top 4, the top three were USA, England and Canada. USA defeated Canada in the semifinal and England in the final, 260–71. And similar to the women's game, global growth in the men's game followed very quickly after that initial world event, and by the time the next Men's Roller Derby World Cup rolls around, in Calgary in the summer of 2016, the number of participating nations will be twenty-two.

What this success meant was that within just over a decade, what had started as an all-woman underground American game had become a global, multicultural sport played by everyone.

So of course, in the roller derby community, which hasn't always been known for its patience, cries went out for inclusion in the Olympics as Leo Seltzer had always wanted. But unfortunately, despite all of this growth, that reality is still a long way off.

The relationship between roller sports and the Olympics is not a new one. FIRS, the Fédération Internationale de Roller Sports, has been lobbying for inclusion in the Olympics for decades. In 1992, roller hockey (a.k.a. rink hockey) was included as a demonstration sport in Barcelona, which remains the only example of quad roller skates being represented at the Games.

From 1992 to 2014, no demonstration sports were included in the Olympics in a move to keep the number of sports under control. There are twenty-five core sports and three floaters, all of which are under review after every Games. Since spaces were opened up after the 2008 axing of a few sports from the Summer Games, there was significant optimism that at the very least inline speed skating could be a demonstration sport in 2016; in the end, it lost out to rugby and golf.

With an already bloated Summer Games reluctant to add any more sports to its roster, inclusion is becoming tougher. But this isn't the only challenge roller derby is facing. Despite the immense – and immensely broad – growth, roller derby remains in its infancy. In many cases the desire and the ability to strap on skates and start a league or a team is far outpacing the development of the infrastructure that the sport needs to flourish at an international level.

First off, for a sport to even be recognized by the International Olympic Committee (IOC), it must adhere to a few conventions:

1. The sport must have an International Federation (IF) that acts as an international governing body and runs world championships.
2. That body must adhere to the Olympics' anti-doping policy.
3. The sport must be played by men in at least seventy-five countries on four continents, and women in forty countries on three continents.

At present, roller derby doesn't even adhere to these three rules for consideration. Many will argue that there is an international governing body in the Women's Flat Track Derby Association. Similarly, the men's game is governed by the Men's Roller Derby Association, which has direct crossover ties with the WFTDA. However, FIRS, the leading international body of roller sports and the one with a relationship with the IOC, actually recognizes the USARS version of roller derby: a comparatively little-played form of the sport that has no participation, nor any recognition, outside of the US. This has led to some tension between the organizations. As FIRS has made motions toward bringing roller derby under its umbrella, the WFTDA, with direct support from the MRDA, has stepped up its attempts to be recognized as the official international governing body of the sport. In October 2015, the association issued simultaneous letters to both FIRS and the IOC laying claim to their position. In the releases, the WFTDA did not rule out working with FIRS, in a rules licensing partnership, for example, but it did assert its autonomy, stating that "the WFTDA will not recognize FIRS as the international governing body of roller derby, nor will we cede the authority to govern and direct the future of roller derby to FIRS. The leagues and skaters that participate in the sport globally – including wom en's and men's roller derby, adult and junior derby – universally acknowledge the WFTDA as the dominant governing body for the sport."

In its letter to the IOC, the WFTDA cited its membership's commitment to democratic athlete-ownership of the game – unprecedented among sport's organizations – and concluded that

> the WFTDA has successfully managed flat track roller derby for a decade. We have developed an effective and strong community of athletes, coaches, and officials, which is capable of governing the sport independently. The WFTDA has the unified support of tens of thousands of athletes, coaches and officials from six continents. We wish to continue to build consensus and leverage that support, allowing those who are involved as experts in the sport to continue to govern independently, democratically and in a unified manner. We are prepared to do whatever we need to in order to comply with IOC guidelines, so long as we are able to protect the integrity and independent governance of our sport.

However, at present neither USARS nor WFTDA/MRDA adheres to the IOC's strict – and incredibly expensive – anti-doping policy, and also confusingly, the WFTDA does not run the women's world championships. The men's World Cup, however, is directly linked to the MRDA, but the women's is run by the for-profit *Blood & Thunder* magazine, albeit with increased collaboration with the WFTDA, to the point where WFTDA executive director Bloody Mary represented the association in both the 2014 Roller Derby World Cup Parade of Nations and the medal ceremony, signifying an increased relationship between the WFTDA and *Blood & Thunder*.

Of course, roller derby doesn't adhere to the current, inherently sexist, gender ratio. To the IOC's defence, roller derby's female-driven rise is nearly unprecedented in the history of competitive sport. It wouldn't be hard to imagine that the members of the IOC would be more than willing to flip those ratios. However, even with the flipped ratios, roller derby still isn't quite there yet, which isn't to say it never will be. Take rugby, for example, one of the planet's oldest, and most popular, team games: it was only granted acceptance for the 2016 Games.

Outside of these technicalities, roller derby still has some internal issues that will have to be dealt with in order for it to be ready for the Olympic spotlight. One of these issues is with the lack of parity in the international game. At the first World Cup there were noticeable tiers, with Team USA in its own stratosphere, England and Canada on a stage of their own and a handful of countries on the next tier – Finland, Sweden, Australia, etc. While parity between the fifth and twelfth seeds increased somewhat in 2014, the unchanged Top 4 remained well ahead of the pack.

There are, however, examples of the IOC overlooking a lack of parity to allow for participation in the hopes that it will fuel growth in the sport. Germany's dominance in luge and the Netherland's dominance in long-track speed skating are good examples, but in comparison to roller derby, women's hockey is the most apt. Canada and the USA are in a league of their own in that sport. Starting in 1998, the first few Olympic tournaments were, to put it bluntly, a joke, much like the men's had been in 1920 and '24. But beginning in 2006, when Sweden upset the US and eventually took home silver, the rest of the world began to catch up. There is still a long way to go, but scores of 3–1 and 4–2 at the 2014 Sochi Winter Olympic Games replaced the 11–1 and 13–0 drubbings that were once commonplace. It was the spotlight of the Olympics that was critical in kick-starting the growth.

Another obstacle that roller derby faces is in defining a consistent rule set. Right now, there is no question that the WFTDA/MRDA rule set is the dominant one in the sport, not to mention the most refined and battle tested. But there are a few competing sets, most notably USARS, but also MADE and OSDA (Old School Derby Association). This plurality essentially only exists in the US and, therefore, is not too big a concern on a global scale, and another look at hockey illustrates that this is an issue that can be dealt with. The International Ice Hockey Federation uses a different sized rink and slightly altered – some would say more strict – rule set from that used in the National Hockey League, yet skaters transition between them all of the time.

So, while the desire is there and the growth is consistent, the sport of roller derby is still a long way off from inclusion in the Olympic Games. But given how much and how quickly the sport has grown in the first decade of its existence, it is not hard to imagine that in another twenty years or so, roller derby could be ready for that brightest of spotlights. Perhaps a bigger question is whether or not this goal is one that is desired by the majority of the skaters playing the game.

The biggest contributor to the growth of the global game may well come from the junior ranks. In 2015, the junior game had grown enough globally to hold its first World Cup in Seattle, Washington, with five countries invited, but only three attending and fielding four coed rosters: Team USA fielded both an East and a West roster to compete against Australia and Canada. With the WFTDA taking over the governance of the junior game in 2015, creating its Junior Flat Track Derby

Association, the established association's infrastructure will help propel growth of the junior game. With the juniors playing under a unified rule set and led by an established, globally relevant organization, many issues will eventually be solved.

Global growth is the new frontier of flat track roller derby. Established and well-rooted in North America, the game has spread internationally like never before, changing the look and feel of the game.

the wide-open track ahead

FLAT TRACK ROLLER DERBY
COMES OF AGE

January 17, 2015. Toronto, ON

It's a cold day. A frigid late afternoon in the midst of Toronto's settling into the heart of winter. I bury my face in my scarf and pick up my pace. My head is tilted downward to deflect the cold wind that cuts across the parking lot, so I watch as each step of my boots ricochets off of the cold asphalt underfoot. There is chatter up ahead, and I risk a glance upwards to see, against the backdrop of a large concrete warehouse, a few huddled packs of smokers, their exhalations hovering motionless above them before dissipating into the air. Near them there is a lineup in front of a food truck, patrons shuffling to keep warm, keeping close together in the line. Then a group of skaters rushes out of a parked car, bursting out of the doors in near unison, gear slung over one shoulder, in some cases skates slung over the other, and they rush toward the entrance, their bare legs looking pale and cold. I follow them up the few steps, through the green metal doors and into a dark, cavernous space, at the end of which is yet another line, this one flanked by security guards who check bags and chat with regulars. The people are being efficiently funnelled through a massive garage-like door. I move past them, skipping the queue, nod to the guards and head inside; suddenly the space opens up and I am hit by the near glow of the whitewashed walls, the busy patter, the flow of bodies, the sound of rock music, the numerous greetings of the numerous people whom I recognize and know. Only then – finally past the hectic entrance and the salutations – do I stop to take it all in. It's been nearly five years, and I'm shocked to discover that this ragged, dusty, pillar-filled and seemingly unworkable bunker has become such a comfortable space.

It's the opening night of Toronto Roller Derby's ninth house-league season, and the fourth full season to be held here in the Bunker, the longest continuous home in ToRD's near-decade-long existence. It is perhaps the most unlikely venue in Canadian roller derby history, but one that has become a fixture on the scene not only in this country, but also in the world. I hated this space when the league first moved here: the false light of the windowless sepulchre, the frustrating geometric contortions needed to fit two tracks inside, the dust filtering in from the set-design workshops and the sound studios that share the building. And while nothing has changed to make it any more hospitable to the sport played within it, it has nonetheless become comforting. It has become home.

Sometimes during the midst of a season, things can happen quickly. Come April, when the house leagues are still in full swing and the travel teams have begun their push toward the fall's playoffs, it becomes impossible to stop and take it all in, reflect on what is happening, how we got here and what direction we're headed in. But at the season opener this sort of reflection – however sentimental – is almost impossible to avoid. Personally, I can't help but think back to my first game and have a hard time believing that it was eight years ago, which in derby years is actually a few lifetimes. That's exactly what it feels like.

You enter the Bunker in the southeast corner of the room, and track 2 is to your immediate left, but on game days it is hidden by a series of temporary walls that portion off the space into dressing rooms and a warm-up area. Fans are directed toward the vendor alley that travels all the way along the east wall and then onto track 1, the game track, which is ringed by metal bleachers. It's packed, as opening night usually is, with the bleachers quickly filling, and the suicide seats already occupied by the lawn chairs of regulars and by the crossed legs of those who don't mind sitting directly on the polished concrete, those who relish the proximity to the track and the opportunity to build beeramids.

I pause at the edge of the track before heading to my favourite spot at the apex of turns 1 and 2: on a track with pillars, being able to see both straightaways is essential for me. There is a buzz in the air; the packed crowd always a relief at the beginning of a new season. Attendance had slipped after 2011, but seemed to bounce back in 2014, a welcome sign that the sport is still entrenched. And studying this crowd, with so many familiar faces, I realize that the fans have not really changed over the years. I did notice during those oh-so-busy days in 2010 how game in and game out I would see a few hundred people regularly, while hundreds of new faces – seemingly different every game – would fill out the crowds. Now, years later, that core has barely wavered, but there are less uninitiated fans around the fringes. The newness has worn off. Somehow, this new reality seems OK, because those people at the core have become real fans. They've become fans of the sport, not gawkers of the spectacle or even just admirers of the lifestyle.

Monichrome, one of my co-announcers, used to always say, half jokingly, that people "came for the skirts, but stayed for the sport." That's never been truer than in the present, even if I haven't seen a real skirt on the track in a long time.

I head over to my corner and reserve some spots for friends who are coming, who have become semi-regulars. This is a rare treat for me, simply watching a game and not calling it. Generally, Toronto's local station Rogers TV shoots the regular season house league games, but the crew is led by the same producer, Brendan Peltier, who shoots the Toronto Marlies. There is a conflict in schedules tonight, and in Canada, hockey always wins, leaving me free to sit back and enjoy the game that I have come to love.

As the first to arrive in our section, I get to take it all in. There is other media here; the regular City TV guys are lurking around the track, getting ready to shoot highlights for the Monday night spot, but I notice that CTV is here as well, preparing for a live piece that will air on the evening news. They are here for the season opener, but also to report on ToRD's search for a new venue. It's a problem that will ironically bring a lot of press ToRD's way in these opening weeks of the season. A positive side effect of a big problem, and one that plagues leagues all over the world: finding an affordable, permanent home. It's hard to believe that these grown-up problems reside at the core of the game now, and that mainstream media is on hand to cover it.[12] Just a few years previous, all of these notions – permanent, full-time facilities; mainstream media attending games – would have seemed impossible. Or alien. But much has changed, and early in 2015, at the beginning of the WFTDA's tenth-anniversary season, the sport seems like it's found a groove.

It had been somewhat of a tumultuous few years for the Women's Flat Track Derby Association. Beginning in 2010, when the flat track game began to evolve in ways distinct from any other version of the game that preceded it, there was push back toward the association from virtually every corner; whether from roller derby's remaining patriarch, Jerry Seltzer; or its bloggers like WindyMan; or even parts of the WFTDA's membership itself. From 2010 to 2013 the sport of flat track roller derby came under attack in ways that would have seemed ludicrous during the all-inclusive love-in that defined the community from 2003 to 2009. Personally, I think people were losing the big picture in the details.

In 2014, I believe flat track roller derby truly came of age. The sometimes awkward adolescence that hobbled the game through its strategic and subsequent rules evolution finally seemed to balance out. The game hasn't changed much over the past two seasons, though of course it has gotten better through refinement, nor have the rules changed, aside from some clarification and tightening. In 2014 we finally got to see what flat track roller derby is going to look like, more or less, from here on in.

Some people still aren't sold on the flat track game, and that's fine, but after an incredible 2014 WFTDA playoff and a heart-warming World Cup, played under the WFTDA rule set, the attacks on the WFTDA seem shallow. They seem to be coming from people who simply don't like the sport, yet still want to be a part of it, perhaps due to reasons of sentimentality or nostalgia: "But that's not what the game looked like when *I* discovered it!"

I've always run against the grain in this regard, as I only truly fell in love with the sport in the fall of 2009 when all the elements that people seemed to hate about flat track first surfaced. A lot of the criticism that had been lobbed at flat track roller derby over the years was that it had become too slow, too much of a grind, too much of a departure from the "purity" of the banked track game. For me, the game of flat track roller derby existed only in name until that point; it was just a version of the banked track game played on a flat surface. Some people were content with this style of play, but logically, thinking that the strategies that defined the banked track would survive forever on the flat one is equivalent to thinking that ice hockey strategies could be transported to field hockey: different surfaces, different games.

In the early, evolutionary days of other sports, similar changes happened. It's quite amazing to think that something as seemingly obvious as allowing forward passing in hockey was met with great controversy when it occurred. First instituted on the west coast (Pacific Coast Hockey Association) in 1913, it took nearly fifteen years for the NHL to finally adopt the strategy and allow passing in all zones (McFarlane, 35).

People, in sports as in all walks of life, fear change first and foremost, before hopefully coming to embrace it.

My friends arrive just in time for the opening whistle; a few of these are long-time friends of Dawson's, going all the way back to high school on the East Coast. And that too reminds me how in my earliest days as a fan of the sport she was the one who would be sitting next to me trackside, as we yelled ourselves hoarse in the suicide seats of Montreal's Arena Saint-Louis. But now, as ToRD's venue announcers Mr. Whistler and Bill Murray – not *that* Bill Murray – introduce the Death Track Dolls, Dawson skates out confidently and excitedly with her teammates. I can't help but feel a swell of pride to see her on the track; this will be her seventh season with the Dolls. It's been quite a journey for her. Since the beginning of her time in ToRD, she has been an active member of the league. She served for three years as vice president through its transitions to two new venues and its growth into a D-1 WFTDA league. She helped found the league's B-travel team, the Bay Street Bruisers, and served as captain for the first two years of its existence. And interestingly, she also quietly became the first skater in ToRD to have only her real name on her jersey, dropping the "Downright Dirty" part of her moniker during her two years on the Bruisers and eventually following suit on the Dolls as well.

At the start of 2015, with less responsibility off the track, she is playing the best derby of her career, able to focus finally on her play. She was a key member of the Dolls' championship run in 2014, its second in a row. Tonight, her team will kick off its title defence against its chief rivals, the Gore-Gore Rollergirls, in a rematch of the previous season's Battle for the Boot.

From the opening whistle, the game is intense. It's tight with leads changing rapidly. My friends, accustomed to the game now, ask less and less questions, better able to understand the sport and its flow. One member of the group is at only his second game and it has been nearly a year since his first, but I am intrigued that he has managed to understand the game so quickly. He has no questions about the action on the track, just questions about the specifics of the rules. As I watch the game unfold, I realize that he gets it so easily, despite being away for a year, because the game itself has not changed much in that time. Now it is what it is. That frantic, constant forward motion of the earlier days of the flat track experiment is gone. Looking back upon video from that time, I'm always struck by how boring the games could be, a slow awkward race. Now the complexity of the pace strategies make it far more dynamic: blazing speed commingled with grinding slowness. It's a fascinating dichotomy to watch play out as two evenly matched teams meet on the track.

At halftime of the season opener, the two teams are within five points of one another and the buzz of the crowd has not dissipated. Everyone is sharing in the excitement of the game and the product on the track. In 2014 there was a big turnover caused by the retirement of some of the league's first generation of skaters. Many are in the crowd, hanging out with the current members of Toronto's charter team, CN Power, who are also in attendance, scoping out future players perhaps, trying to decipher which skaters will become the next generation of travel-team superstars. I wonder what they are feeling, if they are surprised that the league has continued so strongly without them, or if, now that they have a chance to step back and take a look, they see how much the game has changed and how far the sport has come. It's strange and wonderful to see the multiple generations that make up the league and Canadian roller derby in general. In the grand narrative of the sport, Canadian roller derby is truly in the middle of it all, and it seems astonishing to me that 2016 marks the tenth anniversary of the game in our country.

For a long time it seemed as if Canada was constantly playing catch-up, with the game in general, but also with its own dominant league as well, Montreal Roller Derby. In 2014, that changed. Both Toronto and Terminal City pushed the Skids to new heights of competitiveness, and in 2015, the game at the national level was played on an even closer playing field as more and more leagues gained WFTDA Division 1 and 2 experience and learned to play the game at a higher, more athletic level. In the 2014 WFTDA Division 2 Playoffs, for example, Ottawa's Rideau Valley Vixens defeated Berlin's Bear City in an incredible final game of one of the most intense tournaments that flat track roller derby has ever seen. It was hosted by Canada's Tri-City Roller Derby, no less, the first time a Division 2 championship was held outside of the US.[13] Those thrilling D2s were followed by equally thrilling D1 playoffs that were capped off by one of the greatest games ever, when New York's Gotham held off Portland's Rose City (147–144) to retain the Hydra.

Sure, Canada didn't surprise as it did in 2013 when Toronto and Terminal City both went on spirited and unexpected runs in their respective division playoffs, and Montreal once again lived up to its moniker as being the Most Heartbreaking Team in playoff history with another last-gasp loss, this time to long-time rivals Charm City Roller Girls out of Baltimore. Nonetheless it was a banner year for the sport in the country and it saw the rise of a new, true power from the west in the Calgary Roller Derby Association, whose record-setting march up the WFTDA standings has made them a team to watch. Overall, with the additions of St. Albert Heavenly Rollers Derby League in Alberta, the Winnipeg Roller Derby League and Guelph's Royal City Roller Girls, at the beginning of 2015 there were fifteen WFTDA leagues in Canada spread across all three divisions, part of the three hundred member leagues overall.

Globally the game is growing, not only at the national level, as we saw with teams like Argentina and New Zealand at the World Cup, but at the league or club level as well. Berlin, Germany; London, England; and the Victorian Roller Derby League in Melbourne, Australia, all announced themselves as players on the WFTDA circuit. And there are more in the wings. When you think about the struggles and infighting that have gone on in trying to put professional sports leagues like the NHL and the NFL into global markets, the fact that a still-amateur sport like flat track roller derby has been able to sustain a "league" with international membership is nothing short of astonishing.

We settle back into our seats at the end of the break. The second half proves to be as close as the first. In all, the lead will change or the score will be tied at the end of a jam eight times.

However, with only minutes left, the Gore-Gore Rollergirls have built one of the biggest leads of the game, nineteen points, and all seems lost for the Dolls. Dawson's blocking line is on the track for this critical moment. There is maybe time left for two jams if the Dolls use their time outs properly. The jam starts and, with veteran Scarcasm supplying offence, Dawson and her pivot – the tall, striking jammer/pivot Sleeper Hold, who began her career in Toronto's low-contact league – lock in the defence at the back of the pack. They continuously soul crush the Gore's jammer, which entails knocking her out of bounds and then skating backwards, dragging her back along the track, as she must re-enter behind them. Because of this, the pack never moves beyond the first straightaway and the Dolls' jammer makes quick work of the stopped pack: picking up one grand slam for five points, then another and then, as the Gore's jammer finally gets free of Dawson, picking up four additional points before calling it off. The Dolls' bench promptly calls a time out to stop the clock. The score is now 146–141 and there is time for one more jam.

The crowd is standing in unison; Gores fans, Dolls fans, everyone is standing in anticipation of the final jam. The effort of the previous scoring run has sent three of the Dolls' blockers to the penalty box, which means that for this all-important final jam the Gores will have three blockers on the track to the Dolls' one. It doesn't look good for the defending champs. I glance across the track to the penalty box at turn 4 where Dawson sits, having done all she could and sacrificed the penalty to get her jammer through on that final pass to make it this close. I can't help but notice that, although at disparate ends of the track, we are once again back in our regular seats trackside watching the sport we've grown to love together. So despite the tension, I smile at the situation, at the game, at the fact that this once spectacle, then lifestyle movement has grown to a point where it can create these pure sports moments.

The whistle for the final jam goes and as the Gores' pack wraps up the Dolls' jammer, the Gore jammer tries to race through the inside only to get popped out of bounds by the waiting hips of the lone defensive blocker on the track. Both jammers are forced to reset at the back of the pack. Each takes a step back to reassess the situation, and it's almost as if the jam is starting again. The pack seems to sense this and the blockers take a moment to resettle.

On the track, standing side by side, each jammer tenses and you can almost see them seething with anticipation as they peer past the pack of blockers at the wide-open track ahead.

epilogue

In the early morning of Thursday, December 4, 2014, at the Kay Bailey Hutchison Convention Center in Dallas, Texas, a half-awake group of announcers, volunteers and staff was groggily standing in line to check in for credentials at the 2014 *Blood & Thunder* Roller Derby World Cup. Nearby, and snaking all along the interior wall of the cathedral-like mezzanine of the auditorium, were hundreds of fans who'd arrived early to gain entry or pick up last-minute tickets to the event. There was a murmur in the convention center, the buzz of half-formed expectations and fully realized anticipation, but it was muted by the early morning hour, by the remnants of jet lag yet to be shaken.

A set of doors at the near-end of the hall sprang open and out walked Team Argentina, unmistakable to any sports fan in their baby-blue-and-white striped jerseys. With their skates in hand, they were ready for warm-ups for their early morning game on day 1 of the second Roller Derby World Cup.

It took a moment for the groggy mass in the hall to take note of the arrival of the team, but when they did, one part of the

221

sleepy line of fans suddenly erupted: dancing, chanting, singing, flags of Argentina materialized and waved proudly. The singing accompanied the blushing and appreciative team as it entered the World Cup stadium and disappeared from our view.

Yet the singing continued. The dancing continued, and it would do so nearly unabated for the next four days.

It was my first World Cup moment and it proved to be just one of a countless number of World Cup moments that would touch and inspire everyone who gathered in Dallas that year. This event would turn out to be – arguably – flat track roller derby's greatest moment to date, an incredible achievement for a sport only a decade into its very existence.

Two thousand fourteen was quite a year for flat track roller derby, a bounce-back year in many ways for its leading governing body, the WFTDA, through whom virtually all of the participants at the World Cup were introduced to the game. The recently completed 2014 WFTDA playoffs were an incredible success on the track, and globally the game had grown far beyond even the thirty teams in attendance in Dallas. This was made evident by the donations of gear being collected on site for an emerging league in Beirut and the buzz around the newly formed league in Cairo (the CaiRollers). For a potentially defining year in the early history of flat track roller derby, the 2014 World Cup proved to be a fitting end.

No, the World Cup was not a highly competitive tournament, though arguably more competitive than some thought it would be, and no, the dominance of the United States was not negated, though the Americans were tested more than any thought possible. What it was, was a celebration of the sport, a global coming-out party on a scale that far eclipsed that of the inaugural World Cup in Toronto in 2011. Of course, through the sheer force of evolution, this event was way bigger and way better than that previous one, but that is as it should be, and undoubtedly the next event will be way better than this one – though it is hard to see how it could be any bigger, at least in terms of participation. Along with being a wildly celebratory party, it was also, perhaps most importantly, the largest swap meet the sport has ever seen: a sharing of the game, of strategies, of training.

It was hard not to be taken in by the multiplicity of languages being spoken, the national pride displayed in T-shirts, costumes and in the hoarse voices of the fans, some of whom had travelled thousands of kilometres just to see their nations, in some cases, get crushed by the opposition. For a vast majority of the countries who were taking part, for the West Indies and the South Africas and the Puerto Ricos and the Denmarks, just being there was a victory. It was an announcement of what the sport had become. Where it was going.

On the final day of the event, the World Cup moved into the Kay Bailey Hutchison Arena, an eight-thousand-seat arena that would hold a single track and would host the Parade of Nations and the final games of the tournament. It was packed and loud, with the only precedent being the WFTDA Championship tournaments that had been held in similar venues for a few years, most recently in Nashville, but also Milwaukee, Denver and in Chicago in 2010, where big-arena flat track derby truly made its debut.

Now, the game was better than it had ever been, played by stronger and fitter athletes in more places on the planet than anyone could ever have conceived only ten years prior. Growth had not been marked in spectators, but in participants. And in Dallas in December 2014, it finally struck me that this was why this time – as opposed to any other point in the game's history

– the sport would survive. For the first time ever, the sport of roller derby was building from the bottom up. The deep foundation had been poured, and what was needed was patience and positivity.

For all of the spectacle that the Roller Derby World Cup provided, the most profound moment for me came not during the tournament itself, but during an exhibition game on the Sunday right before the bronze and gold medal games. It was a junior coed all-star game featuring skaters from across the United States and two from Toronto Junior Roller Derby. Originally, I, along with most of the people I'd spoken with, shrugged off the exhibition game. Saw it as an opportunity to grab some food or a drink before the "real" games were played. But those who stayed in the crowd – and there were many – were treated to something special.

It was a stunning bout, a shockingly well-skated game, a display of talent by two teams of teenagers who will, in time, change the sport in ways unimaginable. And as word spread of the intensity of the game and the skill level at which it was being played, the venue started to refill.

Sitting in the arena at the convention centre late in that ultra-competitive match, I found myself thinking back to Chicago in 2010, and how mind-blowingly profound that WFTDA Championship weekend had been for me. My revelation at the UIC Pavilion that November was a powerful one, though admittedly vague. I remember thinking with great confidence that the game was bigger than all of us and had reached a point of a certain kind of transcendence; that it would exist and continue on past that event and those people participating in it. But I didn't know or couldn't articulate exactly what that meant at the time. I guess what was unclear about that particular revelation was who it was that would replace us all, carry the game beyond us toward something better. But suddenly in Dallas five years later it made total sense. After eight years following the sport closely, after announcing hundreds of games and writing nearly three hundred thousand words about it, that initial, profound revelation finally had reached a state of clarity.

The future lay in the hands of those women who'd trekked from every corner of six continents of the globe; it lay in the hands of the boys and girls who left fans with jaws agape during that junior all-star game in Dallas. And it finally hit me that not only had the game reached such a point where it wouldn't fade away; it had also become clear that the future of the sport was in good hands.

ACKNOWLEDGEMENTS

First off, I need to thank the skaters. All of them. But in particular, those skaters who have directly allowed me entryway into this sport. There are far too many to name, but I am forever indebted to the women who make up Montreal Roller Derby, Toronto Roller Derby and Durham Region Roller Derby. Montreal introduced me to and then taught me the game, Toronto trusted me to tell its story and provided wonderful opportunities to do so, and Durham Region has continuously reminded me why it's all so important. The trust and opportunity provided to me by these leagues have been invaluable, and it has been inspiring.

I also benefited so much from the hard work and research of many other scholars and writers. I am very much aware of my status as a straight man writing about a predominantly women's sport, so in the chapters about feminism and the LGBTQ+ community in particular, I relied heavily on research and the work of others to shape my narrative. I could not have told this part of the story without them. In particular, the writing of M. Ann Hall, Nancy J. Finley, and Leslie Heywood and Shari Dworkin was especially enlightening. Also editor Melanie Sartore-Baldwin's book of collected essays (by various authors), *Sexual Minorities in Sport*, was absolutely invaluable.

This is also not the first book written about the sport of roller derby. It is a not extensive, but nonetheless growing library of books, and I have tried to read them all. A few in particular have been by my side throughout. I had some preconceived ideas about what roller derby was before the twenty-first century revival, and – I don't mind admitting – most of my impressions were wrong. The process of researching this book has given me the utmost respect for the skaters who built this sport through the twentieth century. Keith Coppage's *Roller Derby to RollerJam* provides a thorough and detailed history of the sport from 1935 to 2000. Frank Deford's beautiful *Five Strides on the Banked Track* is a fantastic bit of sports writing, providing an intimate look into what it was like on the road with "the Roller Derby" during its heyday in the late '60s. I strongly recommend both, particularly for those with an interest in learning about the sport's rich, varied history.

There have, of course, been books written about the revival as well. Melissa Joulwan's *Rollergirl* was an excellent entryway into the deep history of flat track and a good companion piece to the film *Hell on Wheels*, but the best of the bunch is undoubtedly *Down and Derby: The Insider's Guide to Roller Derby* by Jennifer "Kasey Bomber" Barbee and Alex "Axles of Evil" Cohen. I strongly recommend this to any person who wants to get involved in the game. Actually, it should be required reading.

I also want to thank my closest allies in the roller derby community, the announcing community and my Canadian co-announcers in particular: Plastik Patrik and Crankypants for inspiration; Lightning Slim, Captain Lou El Bammo, Monichrome, Mr. Whistler, Jaxalottapus, Johnny Capote, Tipsy McStaggers and innumerable other Canadian voices with whom I've had the pleasure of working over the years. I could probably write a whole book on the exploits of the voices of the game.

I would like to give a special thanks to the team at Wolsak and Wynn: Ashley Hisson, Emily Dockrill Jones, Joe Stacey and Paul Vermeersch, who first approached me with the idea for the book, and in particular the editor (and publisher) of this book, Noelle Allen. I would also like to acknowledge the Ontario Arts Council for their support during the writing of this book.

Finally, I'd like to thank my family. Given the nature of this book, I'd like to especially thank the women in my family, and particularly my sister, Krystal "Hitz" Miller; grandmother Barbara Sheffield; mother, Judy Miller; and my partner, Jan Dawson. Dawson and I found this game with each other and its presence has shaped the second decade of our lives together. I wouldn't have wanted to take this journey with anyone else. This book, quite literally, would not have been possible without her.

NOTES

1 The tournament welcomed Atlantic Canadian teams until 2013 when Moncton would host their own East Coast specific version, The Murder. The West has its own version called Summer Slam that also began in 2013.

2 Babe Ruthless was the derby name of Ellen Page's protagonist in *Whip It*.

3 This would be the only loss that Montreal's New Skids would experience against a Canadian opponent until 2015, and it wasn't even a full-length game. That was a run of seventeen straight wins over six years until Terminal City beat them once again in May 2015 by a narrow score of 182–177.

4 Speaking of playoff heartbreak: Montreal would lose that thrilling game 137–135, in a game that would eventually win DNN's annual Game of the Year award at its end-of-season awards. But that would be little consolation to this Montreal team that would continue to have these heartbreaking playoff moments, eventually culminating in a shocking one-point quarterfinal loss to Baltimore in 2014 (a game they'd led until the very end), a year that would see a massive string of retirements of these first-generation Skids.

5 From the Mad Rollin' Dolls blog:
MRD, pursuant to its mission of promoting women's roller derby, does not and will not discriminate on the basis of race, color, religion (creed), gender expression, age, national origin (ancestry), disability, marital status, sexual orientation, or military status, in any of

its activities or operations. MRD does not and will not differentiate between members who identify as female and those who identify as a non-binary gender (including but not limited to genderqueer, transmasculine, transfeminine, and agender) and does not and will not set minimum standards of femininity for its membership or interfere with the privacy of its members for the purposes of league eligibility. These activities include, but are not limited to, draft/home team skater eligibility, membership eligibility, disbursement of resources, and eligibility for office. MRD is committed to providing an inclusive and welcoming environment for all skaters, officials, volunteers, and fans. (Emily, "Mad Rollin' Dolls roller derby league passes more fully-inclusive non-discrimination policy," October 14, 2014, http://madrollindolls.blogspot.ca/2014/10/mad-rollin-dolls-roller-derby-league.html.)

6   Mr. Force is a play on his wife's derby name, G Force, which is a common occurrence in the game. For example, another announcer in ToRD is Mr. Whistler, a play on his partner's name, Penny Whistler (a referee), and before I became the Derby Nerd, I was known as Downright Dirty Dave, or simply as one of the Dawsons.

7   Bambi didn't make my list, but she could have. Or would have been at the top of the list if I'd named this list The Most Inexplicable Skaters in Canadian Roller Derby History. She was like an elastic band on the track and defied expectations for a derby skater: way too small, too weak, not stable enough on skates, yet at times completely unstoppable and nearly impossible to knock down. Do yourself a favour and go to a computer and to WFTDA.tv, click on the Archives tab and search Toronto Boston (only one game should come up, from the 2013 Division 1 playoffs). Fast-forward to the 59:48 mark of the video and watch what Bambi does here, snaking her way through a pack of Boston blockers. (It's followed by a slo-mo replay, so watch that too.) It's inexplicable: the footwork, the track sense, the audacity. There are very few jammers out there capable of pulling something like that off.

8 Starting in 2005, RollerCon is an annual gathering of the roller derby community in Las Vegas built around a series of skating classes,
off-skates lectures, scrimmages and, to be honest, partying.

9 For the record, Casey concluded that Gotham/Team USA skater
Nicole Williams (a.k.a. Bonnie Thunders) was the LeBron James
of roller derby, a sentiment that would be shared by ESPN.com's
Andy Frye in an article published nearly two years later called
"Meet … The LeBron James of Roller Derby?"

10 2011 All-World Team: Sargentina (Argentina); Nanda (Brazil);
Iron Wench (Canada); Kamikaze Kitten (England); Kata Strofi
(Finland); Sandrine "Francey Pants" Rangeon (France); Heavy Ro-
tation (Germany); Zola Blood (Ireland); Jordan Leah "Skate the
Muss" Parore (New Zealand); Marla Mayhem (Scotland); Swede
Hurt (Sweden); Joy Collision (USA); and the tournament MVP was
Montreal's Smack Daddy.

11 Up to this point, Canada had notched the top performances against
USA, limiting them to two hundred fifty-two points in an exhibition
game in summer 2013 (final score 252–72), and then managing to
grab ninety points from them almost exactly a year later in a 356–
90 loss.

12 In the end, ToRD was able to renew and extend its lease with the
operators of the Bunker for at least a few more years.

13 2014 was the second year of WFTDA Division 2 play, and that particular tournament will go down in history for so many reasons. Off
the track it was the first WFTDA tournament held outside of the
US; on the track it was the first to feature a team from continental
Europe, the first to feature two nations' capitals squaring off (it happened twice, with Berlin facing both DC and Ottawa's Rideau Valley) and the first tournament to feature two non-US combatants in
the final (Berlin vs. Rideau Valley). On the track, it was an incredibly competitive tournament, with the average point differential over
the whole weekend being a measly forty-one points.

BIBLIOGRAPHY

Atwell, Margot. *Derby Life: A Crash Course in the Incredible Sport of Roller Derby*. Brooklyn, NY: Gutpunch Press, 2015.

Barbee, Jennifer, and Alex Cohen. *Down and Derby: The Insider's Guide to Roller Derby*. Berkley, CA: Soft Skull Press, 2010.

Beaver, Travis D. "'By the Skaters, for the Skaters': The DIY Ethos of the Roller Derby Revival." *Journal of Sport and Social Issues* 36, no. 1 (February 2012): 25–49.

Blood on the Flat Track: The Rise of the Rat City Rollergirls. DVD. Directed by Lainy Bagwell and Lacey Leavitt. Toronto: Mongrel Media, 2009.

Borcea, Dana. "Get the Painkillers, Roller Derby's Back." *Hamilton Spectator*, Monday, July 24, 2006.

Buzuvis, Erin E. "Transexual and Intersex Athletes." In Sartore-Baldwin, *Sexual Minorities in Sports*, 55–71.

Casey, Liam. "Roller Derby's Race for Respect." *Toronto Star*, December 1, 2011. http://www.thestar.com/sports/2011/12/01/roller_derbys _race_for_respect.html.

Chananie-Hill, Ruth, Jennifer J. Waldron and Natalie K. Umsted. "Third-Wave Agenda: Women's Flat-Track Roller Derby." *Women in Sport and Physical Activity Journal* 21, no. 1 (Spring 2012): 33–49.

Copland, Simon. "Roller Derby Could Herald a Revolution for Gender Equality in Sport." *The Guardian*, June 18, 2014. http://www .theguardian.com/lifeandstyle/2014/jun/18/could-the-men-of -roller-derby-become-sports-first-male-feminists.

Coppage, Keith. *Roller Derby to RollerJam: The Authorized Story of an Unauthorized Sport*. Santa Rosa, CA: Squarebooks, 1999.

Cunningham, Pamela. "End of an Era: The Oil City Derby Girls Reflect on 8 Years at the Grindhouse." *Derby Frontier* (blog), June 3, 2014. http://derbyfrontier.com/2014/06/03/end-of-an-era-the-oil-city -derby-girls-reflect-on-8-years-at-the-grindhouse/.

Davison, Kevin G., and Blye W. Frank. "Sexualities, Genders and Bodies in Sport: Changing Practices of Inequity." In Young and White, *Sport and Gender in Canada*, 178–93.

Deford, Frank. *Five Strides on the Banked Track: The Life and Times of the Roller Derby*. Boston: Little, Brown, 1971.

Encyclopædia Britannica. "How a Sport Becomes an Olympic Event." In *Encyclopædia Britannica Almanac*, 2006. http://academic.eb.com /olympics/reflections/article-277355.

Epstein, David. *The Sports Gene: Inside the Science of Extraordinary Athletic Performance*. New York: Current, 2013.

Fenway, Meg (a.k.a. Vag Lightning). Personal interview with the author. Toronto: The Bunker, Downsview Park, June 20, 2015.

Finley, Nancy J. "Skating Femininity: Gender Maneuvering in Women's Roller Derby." *Journal of Contemporary Ethnography* 39, no. 4 (August 2010): 359–87.

Fowler, Tanis. "Roller Derby: Full-Contact Sport with all the Frills." *Toronto Star*, April 23, 2011. http://www.thestar.com/sports/2011 /04/23/roller_derby_fullcontact_sport_with_all_the_frills.html.

Frye, Andy. "Grateful Men Riding the Roller Wave." *espnW*, March 13, 2014. http://espn.go.com/espnw/news-commentary/article /10601609/espnw-pioneers-men-roller-derby-credit-women-pav ing-way-inaugural-men-roller-derby-world-cup.

———. "Meet . . . the LeBron James of Roller Derby?" *ESPN*, April 25, 2013. espn.go.com/blog/playbook/fandom/post/_/id/21305/meet -the-lebron-james-of-roller-derby.

———. "Speedy and Shifty, Loren Mutch Leads Pack of New Roller Derby Stars." *espnW*, April 3, 2015. http://espn.go.com/espnw/athletes-life

/article/12610456/speedy-shifty-loren-mutch-leads-pack-new-roller
-derby-stars.

Gender Spectrum. "Understanding Gender." https://www.genderspectrum
.org/quick-links/understanding-gender/.

Grant, Jean. "Ten Couples, Ten Stories: Portraits from a WorldPride Mass Wedding." *Toronto Life*, June 27, 2014. http://torontolife.com /city/ten-couples-share-stories-casa-lomas-mass-wedding-world -pride/.

Hall, M. Ann. "Cultural Struggle and Resistance: Gender, History, and Canadian Sport." In Young and White, *Sport and Gender in Canada*, 56–74.

Hart, Lauren (a.k.a. Sister Disaster), and Jeff Welch (a.k.a. Tipsy Mc-Staggers). Personal interview with the author. Ottawa: Hart and Welch residence, June 21, 2013.

Hell on Wheels: The True Tale of All Girl Roller Derby, Texas Style. DVD. Directed by Bob Ray. Austin: CrashCam Films, 2008. http://www .hellonwheelsthemovie.com/filmmakers.htm.

Heywood, Leslie, and Shari L. Dworkin. "Sport as the Stealth Feminism of the Third Wave." In *Built to Win: The Female Athlete as Cultural Icon*, 25–54. Duluth: University of Minnesota Press, 2003.

Hugs and Bruises: The Story of the Hammer City Roller Girls. Vimeo. Joe Krumins, 2010. https://vimeo.com/33703980.

International Olympic Committee. "The Organisation: Mission." http:// www.olympic.org/about-ioc-institution.

———. *Olympic Charter*. Lausanne, Switzerland: International Olympic Committee, 2015. http://www.olympic.org/Documents/olympic _charter_en.pdf.

"Joker Rollermen Win Skating Cup." *Ubyssey*, February 27, 1947. http://www.library.ubc.ca/archives/pdfs/ubyssey/UBYSSEY _1947_02_27.pdf.

"Jokers Staging Intramural Skating Derby Tomorrow." *Ubyssey*, February 25, 1947. http://www.library.ubc.ca/archives/pdfs/ubyssey /UBYSSEY_1947_02_25.pdf.

Joulwan, Melissa. *Rollergirl: Totally True Tales From the Track.* New York: Touchstone, 2007.

"Justice Feelgood Marshall" [Tracy Williams]. "2009 Nationals: Capsule Recaps." *Derby News Network*, November 14, 2009. http://www.derbynews.net/2009/11/14/2009_nationals_capsule_recaps/.

Konner, Linda. *Roller Fever!: The Complete Book of Roller Skating.* New York: Scholastic, 1979.

Kwasny, Alyssa (a.k.a. Georgia W. Tush). Email interview with the author. July 2014.

Lepperd, Tom, ed. *Official Baseball Rules.* 2015 Edition. New York: Office of the Commissioner of Baseball, 2015. http://mlb.mlb.com/mlb/downloads/y2015/official_baseball_rules.pdf.

"Local Oil City Rollers Hoping for a Roller Derby Renaissance." *Edmonton Journal*, March 20, 2006. http://www.canada.com/edmontonjournal/news/story.html?id=1147aa36-3a52-4a64-9613-5c5b0e8faf20&k=59534.

Mabe, Catherine. *Roller Derby: The History and All-Girl Revival of the Greatest Sport on Wheels.* Denver: speck press, 2007.

Mackin, Bob. "East Sider likes to Skate, Rattle and Roll." *Vancouver Courier*, September 15, 2002. http://www.rollergirl.ca/media/images/misc/courier-article.jpg.

McFarlane, Brian. *50 years of Hockey: An Intimate History of the National Hockey League.* Toronto: Pagurian Press, 1967.

McMullen, Alyson (a.k.a. Kandy Barr). Personal interview with the author. Toronto: McMullen residence, June 23, 2014.

Melton, E. Nicole. "Women and the Lesbian Stigma." In Sartore-Baldwin, *Sexual Minorities in Sports*, 11–29.

Men's Roller Derby Association. "MRDA Non-Discrimination Policy." http://www.mensrollerderbyassociation.com/resources/mrda-non-discrimination-policy/.

Messner, Michael A. *Out of Play: Critical Essays on Gender and Sport.* Albany: State University of New York Press, 2007.

Mitchell, Monica (a.k.a. Monichrome). Personal interview with the author. Toronto: Victory Cafe, June 19, 2014.

National Basketball Association. *Official Rules of the National Basketball Association, 2013–2014.* New York: National Basketball Association, 2013. http://www.nba.com/media/dleague/1314-nba-rule-book.pdf.

National Hockey League. *Official Rules, 2014–2015.* New York: National Hockey League, 2014. http://www.nhlofficials.com/_files/_pdf_2014/2014-2015-Rules-Digital-Final.pdf.

Parker, Melissa, and Philip White. "S/He Plays Sport: Theorizing the Sport/Gender Process." In Young and White, *Sport and Gender in Canada*, 4–31.

Phillips, Ann-Victoria. *The Complete Book of Roller Skating.* New York: Workman, 1979.

Rogers, Injure. "The Vagine Regime: Fracture Interview with Injure Rogers aka The Matron of Muff." By Switchblade Siouxsie. *Fracture Mag*, December 6, 2008. http://www.fracturemag.com/derby/features/vagine-regime (site discontinued).

"Roller Derby Notes" [WindyMan]. "Roller Derby History & Game Fundamentals – 'Another Derby' Seminar." RollerCon 2013 Seminar, filmed August 2, 2013. YouTube video, 1:15:42. Posted August 17, 2013. https://www.youtube.com/watch?v=7rvbheW0d7U&feature=youtu.be.

Rollergirls. TV. Produced by Gary and Julie Auerbach. New York: A&E Television Network, 2006.

Sartore-Baldwin, Melanie L., ed. *Sexual Minorities in Sports: Prejudice at Play.* Boulder, Colorado: Lynne Rienner, 2013.

Schroeder, Norma Carnes. "Micajah C. Henley." WayNet. http://www.waynet.org/people/biography/henley.htm

Seltzer, Jerry. "Jerry Seltzer 2010 WFTDA Champs." By D.D. Miller. The 2010 Women's Flat Track Derby Association Championships, filmed November 7, 2010. YouTube video, 6:10. Posted November 18, 2010. https://www.youtube.com/watch?v=V-em3QNXFdE.

———. Personal interview with the author. Chicago: UIC Pavilion, November 7, 2010.

———. "The World Cup, Just Indescribable." *RollerDerbyJesus.com* (blog), December 8, 2014. https://rollerderbyjesus.com/2014/12/08/the -world-cup-just-indescribable/.

"Sour Cherry" [Sherry Bontkes]. "OCDG History." *Oil City Derby Girls* (blog), March 12, 2008. https://oilcityderbygirls.wordpress. com/2008/03/12/ocdg-history/.

Spencer, Amy. *DIY: The Rise of Lo-Fi Culture*. London: Marion Boyars, 2005.

Storms, Carolyn E. "'There's No Sorry in Roller Derby': A Feminist Examination of Identity of Women in the Full Contact Sport of Roller Derby." *The New York Sociologist* 3 (2008): 68–86.

Suggitt, Lisa. (a.k.a. Rollergirl). Personal interview with the author. Vancouver: RollerGirl store, November 6, 2014.

Symons, Caroline. "The Gay Games." In Sartore-Baldwin, *Sexual Minorities in Sports*, 87–113.

Tate, Dan. "Micajah C. Henley." *Dan Tate's Blog*. https://waynecountyhistory .wordpress.com/2009/10/15/micajah-c-henley/.

Terminal City Rollergirls. "Media Kit." 2009. http://www. terminalcityrollergirls.com/files/TCRG-Media%20Kit%2009.pdf.

This is How I Roll. DVD. Directed by Kat Vecchio. New York: Fork Films, 2012. http://www.thisishowirollmovie.com/.

Wilson, Brian. "Oppression is the Message: Media, Sport Spectacle, and Gender." In Young and White, *Sport and Gender in Canada*, 212–33.

Women's Flat Track Derby Association. "Roller Derby Demographics: Results from the Third Annual Comprehensive Data Collection on Skaters and Fans." March 2012. http://wftda.com/files/roller- derby-demographics-2012.pdf.

———. *The Rules of Flat Track Roller Derby*. TX: Women's Flat Track Derby Association, 2014. https://wftda.com/rules/20141201.

———. "WFTDA Adopts Gender Policy." April 18, 2011. https://wftda .com/news/wftda-adopts-gender-policy.

———. "WFTDA Broadens Protections for Athlete Gender Identity." November 10, 2015. https://wftda.com/news/wftda-broadens-protections-for-athlete-gender-identity.

———. "WFTDA Letter to IOC October 2015." October 7, 2015. http://static.wftda.com/letters/WFTDA-Letter-to-IOC-October-2015.pdf.

———. "WFTDA Membership Announces Launch of Junior Flat Track Derby Association." September 8, 2015. http://wftda.com/news/wftda-membership-announces-launch-of-junior-flat-track-derby-association.

———. "WFTDA Response to FIRS October 2015." October 7, 2015. http://static.wftda.com/letters/WFTDA-Response-to-FIRS-October-2015.pdf.

———. "WFTDA Signs Deal to Stream 2015 Championships with ESPN3." August 7, 2015. http://wftda.com/news/wftda-signs-deal-to-stream-2015-championships-with-espn3.

Young, Kevin, and Philip White, eds. *Sport and Gender in Canada*. 2nd ed. Toronto: Oxford University Press Canada, 2007.

Zanin, Andrea. "Rocking the Rink: Roller Derby Mania Hits Montreal." *Mirror* 22, no. 35 (February 22–28, 2007). http://mtlrollerderby.com/wp-content/pdf/mirror.pdf.

Zimmerman, Kate. "RollerGirl." *National Post*, October 18, 2003. http://www.rollergirl.ca/media/images/misc/national-post.gif.

D. D. MILLER is originally from Nova Scotia but has lived, worked and studied all across Canada. His work has appeared in a number of journals and anthologies, and his first book, *David Foster Wallace Ruined My Suicide and Other Stories*, was published by Wolsak & Wynn's Buckrider Books imprint in 2014. As the Derby Nerd, Miller is known for his writing and commentary on roller derby. He worked as an announcer at both the 2011 and 2014 Roller Derby World Cups and was part of ESPN's broadcast crew for the 2015 WFTDA Championships.

A graduate of Mount Allison University, the University of Victoria and the University of Guelph (where he completed his MFA), Miller currently lives in Toronto, where he teaches in the English Department at Humber College.